craft **workshop**

felt crafts

craft **workshop**

felt crafts

a practical guide in 25 step-by-step original projects
and over 250 photographs

Victoria Brown

southwater

*To Zachary, who was with me
every step of the way, and to
Tom and Mike with love.*

This edition is published by Southwater

Southwater is an imprint of Anness Publishing Ltd
Hermes House, 88–89 Blackfriars Road, London SE1 8HA
tel. 020 7401 2077; fax 020 7633 9499
www.southwaterbooks.com; info@anness.com

© Anness Publishing Ltd 1996, 2005

UK agent: The Manning Partnership Ltd
6 The Old Dairy, Melcombe Road, Bath BA2 3LR
tel. 01225 478444; fax 01225 478440
sales@manning-partnership.co.uk

UK distributor: Grantham Book Services Ltd
Isaac Newton Way, Alma Park Industrial Estate
Grantham, Lincs NG31 9SD
tel. 01476 541080; fax 01476 541061
orders@gbs.tbs-ltd.co.uk

North American agent/distributor: National Book Network
4501 Forbes Boulevard, Suite 200, Lanham, MD 20706
tel. 301 459 3366; fax 301 429 5746; www.nbnbooks.com

Australian agent/distributor: Pan Macmillan Australia
Level 18, St Martins Tower, 31 Market St, Sydney, NSW 2000
tel. 1300 135 113; fax 1300 135 103
customer.service@macmillan.com.au

New Zealand agent/distributor: David Bateman Ltd
30 Tarndale Grove, Off Bush Road, Albany, Auckland
tel. (09) 415 7664; fax (09) 415 8892

A CIP catalogue record for this book is available from the
British Library.

Publisher: Joanna Lorenz
Senior Editor: Lindsay Porter
Photographer: Tim Imrie
Step Photographer: Lucy Tizard
Stylist: Fanny Ward
Designers: Peter Butler and Susannah Good
Illustrators: Madeleine David and Vana Haggerty

The publishers would like to thank the following for the use
of additional images: pp8 left and 9, Trillium Stock, © Cary
Wolinsky; p 8 right, Bridgeman Art Library

Previously published as *New Crafts: Feltwork*

1 3 5 7 9 10 8 6 4 2

CONTENTS

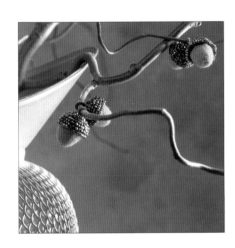

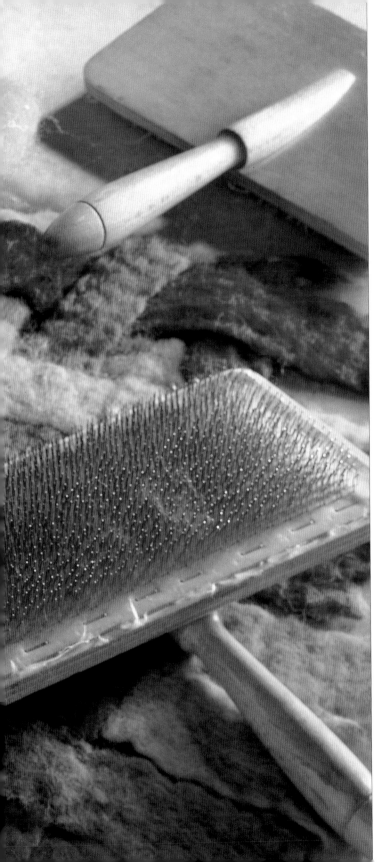

INTRODUCTION

THE MAGIC OF TRANSFORMING FLEECE INTO FELT HAS INSPIRED CRAFTS PEOPLE AND DESIGNERS TO EXPERIMENT WITH A WIDE RANGE OF EFFECTS TO PRODUCE TRULY ORIGINAL PIECES. WHETHER YOU ARE DRAWN TO TRADITIONAL MILLINERY, OR WISH TO EXPERIMENT WITH MORE UNUSUAL EFFECTS, TO CREATE ABSTRACT WALL HANGINGS OR SEAMLESS GARMENTS, THE 25 PROJECTS IN THIS BOOK PROVIDE A COMPLETE COLLECTION OF BEAUTIFUL ITEMS TO MAKE, AND THE GALLERY OF WORK BY CONTEMPORARY DESIGNERS OFFERS FURTHER INSPIRATION FOR EXPLORING THE CRAFT.

Left: Untreated fleece can be transformed into practical and decorative items such as this tea cosy and woven mat.

HISTORY OF FELT

FELT IS A STRANGE AND UNIQUE FABRIC. IT HAS NO WARP OR WEFT, LIKE WOVEN FABRICS, NO RIGHT OR WRONG SIDE, NO BEGINNING AND NO END. IT IS MADE WITH THE MINIMUM OF EQUIPMENT, YET A STRANGE ALCHEMY OCCURS BETWEEN WOOL, MOISTURE, HEAT AND FRICTION, TO CREATE A FABRIC WHICH IS WARM AND HARD-WEARING. IT CAN BE FINE ENOUGH TO DRAPE IN HEAVY FOLDS, OR OF SUCH DENSITY AND THICKNESS THAT IT CAN TAKE ON A SCULPTURAL QUALITY. IT CAN BE LEFT IN ITS NATURAL HUES, OR DYED WITH ALL THE BRILLIANCE OF THE RAINBOW.

Every age and culture seems to have its own myths and legends as to the origins of felt. Yet all the stories contain the correct formula for creating the fabric. In Europe, St Clement and St Feutre are both credited with the discovery of felt, when, according to legend, they each went on a pilgrimage wearing new sandals, which they packed with sheep's wool to ease their blisters. In the Middle East the footsore traveller is a camel driver who took soft camel hair to line his shoes. All these travellers found at the end of their journeys dense mats of felt in their shoes.

Noah is attributed with making what must be the largest piece of felt, when he lined the ark with sheep's fleece. After forty days and nights adrift, the warmth, moisture and movement of the animals produced a thick felt cover for the floor.

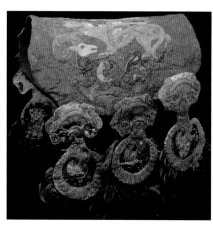

Above: Ornately decorated felt saddle cover, discovered in the frozen tomb at Pazyryk.

The best legend of discovery must be the Persian version. King Solomon's son thought that fleece would make a warm fabric. He sheared the sheep and set about trying to make the wool stick together, without much success. He was so frustrated with his efforts that he burst into tears, and jumped up and down on the fleece. Eureka! He had discovered felt.

Today, the legend of discovery has us all as the central character – who has not put a favourite jumper in the washing machine, to find it shrunk beyond all recognition and stiff as a board?

The use of felt pre-dates all other textiles. Felted animal hair found at Çatal Hüyük in Turkey dates from the Neolithic period (6500 – 6300 BC). The most interesting examples of early felt are from the frozen tombs in the Altai mountains in Siberia. The Pazyryk mounds were preserved by the permafrost and lack of air. Discovered were huge pictorial wall hangings, swans made from fine felt and stuffed with deer hair, beautiful saddle covers trimmed with leather, fur, hair and gold, and other highly decorated items such as floor coverings and cushions. All the pieces are richly coloured, skilfully made and remarkably sophisticated. The most stunning piece in the tomb is the Pazyryk Felt, a huge wall hanging measuring 4.5 x 6.5 m (5 x 7 yd). It shows in repeat pattern the Goddess Tabiti or Apai seated and holding a sacred branch in her hand. In front of her is a man on horseback; he is smaller in size and

Above: Portrait of Federigo da Montefeltro, Duke of Urbino, by Piero della Francesca c.1465. The sitter wears a hand-blocked felted hat typical of the period. Many milliners working today use techniques and styles that are based on Renaissance precedents.

elaborately elegant, with a short, floating cloak and a smooth moustache. The wall hanging is the focus of the Pazyryk collection which is housed in the Hermitage Museum in St Petersburg.

Today, felt is widely known as carpet underlay, fuzzy felt, and the material for hats, piano key pads and the tips of pens. More recently handmade felt has become recognized as an art and craft medium. Its history, however, belongs with the nomads of Central Asia who have used felt in many forms, and who have made felt for over 2,500 years. Felt was so fundamental in the lives of the nomads that the Chinese called their territory in 400 BC "the land of felt". Ghengis Khan referred to the nomads he ruled as "the generations that lived in felt".

The Mongolians not only lived in round felt tents known as yurts, they also had felt structures on top of the carts and wagons in which they travelled. The yurt is an impressive feature of the ancient nomadic life and the tradition has survived to the present day. The yurt is characterized by a freestanding, ridged, domed wooden frame. In the centre of the domed roof there is an opening, as a fire is always lit in the centre of the floor. Although the felts for the tent are white at first, the smoke from the fire gradually changes them first to a peat colour, and

finally to black. The smoke eventually makes the felt brittle and it has to be replaced after five years.

The ancient Mongolians used felt in their daily religious life. Each yurt had felt idols made by the women. These idols were known as the brother of the master and the brother of the mistress, and between these two figures was a third, smaller one, known as the keeper of the house. Although these idols are found in contemporary yurts their true significance has been lost.

Another survivor of the nomadic skill in feltmaking is the kepenek, a cloak made by Turkish shepherds. The kepenek is felted as a single piece using a basic resist, and is used by shepherds as coat, blanket and tent. They are so thick and sturdy they will stand unsupported, and have no decoration. These cloaks evolved from an

earlier garment with sleeves, but it became a sign of status to wear the coat over the shoulders. As this became more and more popular, the sleeves became unnecessary, until they were made sealed, and flapped either side of the cloak like the wings of a flightless bird.

The story of felt past and present is as tangled as the fibres of the fabric. Felt is still made today in the same way that it would have been made 2,000 years ago, and the most effective way of making it is still the simplest. Felt is truly a timeless, and for many a magical, substance.

Below: Felt wall hanging from the tomb at Pazyryk, showing the Goddess Tabiti or Apai, seated holding a sacred branch.

GALLERY

FELT IS AN ANCIENT FABRIC WHICH HAS ENJOYED A REVIVAL IN RECENT YEARS, AND AS MORE PEOPLE BECOME INTERESTED IN USING THE MEDIUM, SO NEW TECHNIQUES ARE PIONEERED. THE WORK SHOWN ON THESE PAGES IS REPRESENTA- TIVE OF CONTEMPORARY FELTMAKING, AND SHOWS THE DIVERSE NATURE OF THE FABRIC AND HOW DIFFERENT DESIGNERS HAVE EXPLORED THE INHERENT QUALITIES OF THE MATERIAL.

Above: FELT BALLS
The marvellous range of colours available in felt can be used to great effect, as illustrated by this collection of felt balls.
VICTORIA BROWN

Right: CONCENTRICITY
This vibrant wall hanging is made from patterned hand-rolled felt, which has been cut and hooked. The combination of hooking the felt and the intense colour gives the piece a richness of pattern reminiscent of mosaics.
MAUREEN SQUAIR

Left: PEAR BLANKET
This piece is made with an inlay technique. The pears and leaves were cut from very soft sheets of handmade felt which were then laid onto brown fleece. The pattern is then felted into the fleece, allowing the design to show distinctly.
ANNE BELGRAVE

Above: DOOR CURTAIN
This colourful design was influenced by the fabric door hangings of India.
VICTORIA BROWN

Left: FOSSILED BOUNDARIES
The depth of vibrant colour in this piece was obtained by using acid dyes and hard carding. Printed silk and silk fibres were embedded in the felting process, and the piece was further enhanced by appliqué, hand- and machine-stitching and printed dyes.
JEANNETTE APPLETON

Below: WALL HANGING
This is a detail of a wall hanging which has been made using the industrial process of needle-punching felt. The fibres are passed between two beds of needles which mat them into the felt.
This allows the artist great control, and very fine details can be achieved.
SAVITHRI BARTLETT

Right: THE STAGE IS SET
The hand-rolled felt used in this piece is very thick, which means that it can be stitched by hand and machine to create a relief effect.
DEE LINTON

Below: APPLE AND SCISSORS
The subtle use of colours and the painterly way the wool fibres have been laid out give this still life a timeless quality. The felt has been made in the traditional way, and the finished effect depends upon the careful preparation of the fibres and slow, methodical hardening and fulling of the felt.
HEATHER BELCHER

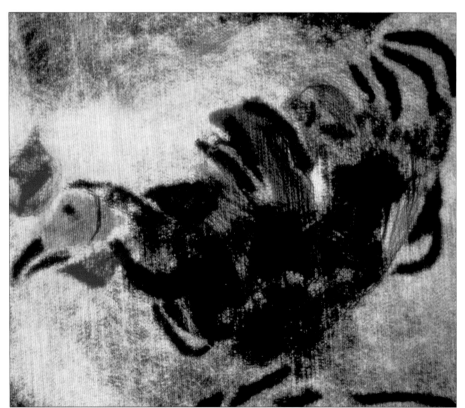

Left: HAT
This wonderful creation has been made with stiffened commercial felt sewn with nylon fibre. The precision and geometry of the hat design is complemented by the flatness of the felt, which in turn inspired the construction of the hat.
MAYU YOSHIKAWA

Above: UNTITLED
These pieces have been machine knitted in fine wool and gently felted or milled. The choice of fine wool makes the pieces lose their knitted appearance, but allows the pieces to retain their flexibility. This technique produces unique surfaces and textures.
LISA SKELTON

Right: WAISTCOAT
This piece was made from hand-rolled felt, and incorporates wool lurex and netting into the surface decoration of the felt. The felt was then cut and pieced together to add further richness to the surface, before being made into the waistcoat.
MAUREEN SQUAIR

Above: WHAT A CREATION
This piece was inspired by early illuminated manuscripts. It is made with hand-dyed commercial felt, and inlaid in a manner similar to wood marquetry. Further embellishments are added with silk embroidery and beads.
STEPHANIE GILBERT

Left: SLIPPERS
These delightful jester slippers were made using a mould, so they are seamless. Wellington boots are ideal moulds for this purpose.
EWA KUNICZAK

Above: MACHINE-
KNITTED COAT
This wonderful coat is
made from machine-
knitted wool, which is
then felted in the washing
machine. All the pieces are
then assembled and
machine appliquéd. Hand
embroidery adds to the
wealth of texture.
TERESA SEARLE

Above: LACE PANEL
Felt is not usually thought
of as a delicate fabric. This
piece combines a web of
flax felted into the lace, to
produce a piece which is
deceptively fragile
looking, but is actually
very robust.
AMANDA CLAYTON

Left: WALL HANGING
(DETAIL)
A colourful example of
the effects that can be
achieved when using
hand-rolled felt.
VICTORIA BROWN

MATERIALS

Most of the materials for feltmaking are available through spinning and weaving suppliers who are always happy to post an order. Wool is the most common fibre for feltmaking, but it can be mixed with other fibres such as silk, flax and mohair. Some animal hair, such as camel hair, will felt very well; others, such as rabbit will not felt unless chemically treated.

Beads Beads are available in a wide range of sizes and shapes and many different materials, including glass, plastic and wood. They can be used to decorate finished items.

Carded wool, sliver This is also known as wool tops and roving. The sliver is wool which has been commercially sorted so that the fibres are of the same length. It is bleached to make it white – this is ideal if you want to dye the wool, especially in clear bright colours. After bleaching the wool is carded into a long rope when it is ready for spinning or the felting. Some people find the wool sliver a bland fibre to use, it is however ideal for the beginner, as so much of the preparation has already been done. Carded sliver always makes a good piece of felt in a reasonable time. It can be brought pre-dyed or it is possible to dye it yourself.

Commercial felt This felt is available in a vast range of colours. The felt is very thin and is not made from pure wool. It can be a useful and versatile fabric, especially as it can be brought off the roll and is therefore very wide.

Embroidery threads These can be bought in many different colours. They can be used to embellish the felt with embroidery or to make tassels.

Felted knitting This can either be knitted by hand or with a knitting machine. Different fabrics can be made by experimenting with different wools and knitting tensions. To felt the fabric, either put it in the washing machine or mill it by hand in alternate hot and cold water, with soap. Wool labelled "machine washable" will not felt.

Felteen This is a clear fabric stiffener which is used on felt hats. The felteen soaks into the felt, making it stiff.

Knitting wool Wool can be used as an inlay pattern with the fleece or used for embroidery prior to the feltmaking. Knitting wool is often appropriate for sewing felt and for making loops and tassels or other finishes.

Lace Lace, netting and other loose-weave fabrics can be incorporated into the felt either for decoration or to strengthen and stabilize the felt.

Metallic threads These threads are available in many colours as well as shades of gold, bronze and silver. Metallic thread can be used to embroider finished felt or it can be trapped under a thin web of fleece and felted into the fabric.

Sewing threads These are used for stitching felt together when the stitches are not to be seen. When it is used on the sewing machine it can make an embossed line or relief effect on the felt.

Uncarded fleece Each breed of sheep has wool with different characteristics. The ideal wool for feltmaking is Merino. Felt is most easily made with the wool that has a staple length (length of the fibre) of about 2.5–5 cm (1–2 in). Shorter fibres make a very dense felt, but they are more difficult to handle. If the fibre is very long and coarse, the fibres will tangle rather than felt. Fleece straight from the sheep's back needs more preparation of the fibres but it gives greater scope for experimentation.

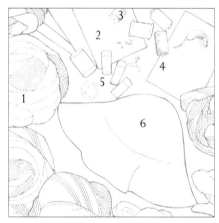

1 Carded wool
2 Commercial felt
3 Metallic threads
4 Sewing threads
5 Beads
6 Wool felt hood

Wool felt hood These are the felts used by milliners for blocking hats. They are available in two sizes; a cone for smaller fitted hats and a capeline for a hat with a brim. Felt hoods are also available in fur felt which is made from rabbit hair and has a glossy finish. Wool felt is matt. The colours available follow the current fashion trends.

Woven wool fabric Tweeds, wool blankets and suiting cloth, are traditionally milled or fulled (felted) after they are woven. This tightens the weave and gives the fabric a smooth finish. Such fabrics can be shrunk further by felting.

EQUIPMENT

FELT MADE FROM CARDED SLIVER CAN BE MADE WITH NO SPECIALIST EQUIP-MENT; ANY OTHER EQUIPMENT NEEDED CAN BE IMPROVISED. THE MOST IMPORTANT ITEM IS A CLOTH OR MAT TO ROLL THE FELT IN; TRY MAKING FELT WITH BOTH AND CHOOSE THE ONE YOU PREFER. IN MONGOLIA, AN OLD FELT, CALLED THE "MOTHER" IS USED TO ROLL THE NEW FELT, WHICH IS CALLED THE "DAUGHTER". LEATHER AND SEA GRASS MATS ARE USED IN OTHER PARTS OF THE WORLD.

Bamboo mat A bamboo or a sea grass beach mat can be used to hold the fleece during felting. The movement of the individual pieces of bamboo when rolled on the fibres increases the friction and speeds the felting process.

Bowl A stainless steel bowl or enamelled bowl is needed for dyeing the wool. Any bowl can be used to mix soap and water.

Calico A pre-washed calico cloth or an old cotton sheet is the most readily available form of backing cloth for rolling the felt. Use a cloth that is bigger than the laid out fleece so that the edges can be turned over the felt.

Drum carder A drum carder will card a large amount of wool quite quickly and efficiently. It is however an expensive piece of equipment to buy unless you are hooked on feltmaking. It is sometimes possible to hire a drum carder for doing larger projects.

Felting tray This is a very useful piece of equipment if the felt is made indoors on a table top as it will contain the water. Fleece can also be laid directly in the tray and with no backing cloth. Photographic, cat litter and some gardening trays are all suitable for felting. If no felting tray is used, work on a draining board, in the shower or outside to prevent the water from dispersing.

Hand carders Once you get into the rhythm of carding, the wool can be prepared quite quickly. If you really hate carding or cannot lay your hands on a pair, use pre-carded wool sliver which can be teased open with your hands.

Jug A jug is useful for pouring hot soapy water over the wool fleece and for mixing dye paste.

Needles A large collection of needles ranging from fine to large bobbin needles is always very useful. For sewing felt choose "straw" needles size/no 5 to 10. A very large needle that can be threaded with wool and has a sharp point is particularly useful for threading felt balls and beads.

Rolling pin Rolling pins can be made from a broom handle, wooden dowel, or even plastic drainage pipe. Use a rolling pin of an appropriate proportion to the felt you are making. If the felt is to be wrapped in cloth to be rolled, the rolling pin needs to be at least the same width as the laid out fleece.

Scissors A variety of scissors are useful for different projects. Large dressmaker's shears should be used for cutting flat felt and commercial felt. Small sharp scissors are for appliqué and embroidery. All scissors need to be kept sharp to cut through the felt smoothly.

Soap flakes All soap will make felt, but different soaps have properties less advantageous to the felt maker. For example, washing-up liquid is mild but is designed to produce a lot of bubbles and it is difficult to wash out. Powder for automatic washing machines does not produce enough bubbles and is very harsh on your skin. Hand soap washes out too quickly. Pure soap flakes are the most suitable as they are very mild and are easy to rinse out.

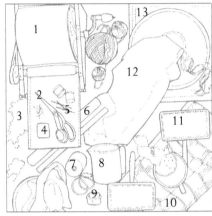

1 Drum carder	8 Jug
2 Scissors	9 Wool brush
3 Soap flakes	10 Bamboo mat
4 Tailor's chalk	11 Hand carder
5 Needles	12 Calico
6 Rolling pin	13 Felting tray
7 String	

Scalpel or craft knife A knife with a sharp blade is essential to cut through felt balls.

String Any string will do as long as it will not disintegrate in hot water. Cotton string is the best to use as the knots will not slip and it can be re-used many times.

Tailor's chalk Tailor's chalk enables you to draw directly onto the fabric. When the marks are no longer needed they can be rubbed off.

Wool brush A teasle or wool brush can be used on the felt to brush up the surface and give it a pile.

BASIC TECHNIQUES

THE TRANSFORMATION OF A MASS OF LOOSE WOOL FIBRES INTO SOLID FELT IS A MYSTERIOUS AND INTRIGUING PROCESS, AS IT REQUIRES ONLY HEAT, MOISTURE AND FRICTION, AIDED BY SOAP. IT COULD BE THE VERY SIMPLICITY OF THE PROCESS THAT HAS INSPIRED NOMADIC TRIBES TO ATTRIBUTE ALMOST MAGICAL PROPERTIES TO THE FABRIC. NO TWO FELT MAKERS WILL USE THE SAME TECHNIQUE, BUT ALL FELT REQUIRES THOSE BASIC INGREDIENTS FOR THE ALCHEMY TO WORK.

PREPARING THE WOOL

Most of the projects in the book have been made with wool which has been industrially cleaned, whitened, carded, and sometimes pre-dyed. This is known as carded sliver. If wool is used straight from the sheep's back, it must be cleaned and carded at home.

1 To clean the fleece, tease it with your hands to remove the larger bits of debris. Dissolve soap flakes in a bowl of lukewarm water. Gently submerge the wool, covering it completely with the water. Let it stand for 15 minutes. Lift the wool out, and replace the dirty water with clean lukewarm water. If the wool needs to be cleaned further, add soap flakes as before and soak again. When the wool is clean, resubmerge it in clean lukewarm water to rinse. Allow the wool to soak, but avoid moving the fleece in the water to prevent it from felting.

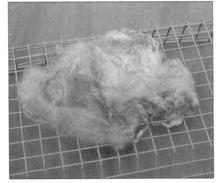

2 Dry the wool in a warm airy place, to allow the air to circulate around it, but away from direct heat.

3 To dye fleece or wool sliver, mix your dye with water, and add to a dye bath of hot water. Follow the manufacturer's instructions for making up the dye. Lower the wool into the dye, making sure the water has not become too hot.

4 Slowly bring the water to the boil, and allow the wool to simmer for an hour, or until all the dye has transferred to the wool, and the water is clear. Do not stir or prod the wool, as this will cause felting. Allow the dye bath to cool before lifting out the dyed wool, and drying it in a warm place as before.

5 Carded sliver can be dip-dyed by holding short sections of the wool in a succession of different dye baths, starting with the lightest colour. The colours can be overlapped to give a wider range of shades.

CARDING

To make an even, strong piece of felt you have to brush out the wool fibres, so that they all lie in the same direction. This is known as carding, and can be done either by hand, or with a piece of equipment called a drum carder.

Hand carding

1 Tease the wool by gently pulling it apart to loosen the fibres. To card the wool, rest the left-hand carder on your knee, and lay small pieces of teased wool on the carding cloth, catching the teeth about 1 cm/¹/₂ in from the top. The fleece may extend over either side of the carder. Fill the carder with a thin, even layer of wool all the way across.

2 Draw the right-hand carder teeth-down across the left-hand carder. Give sufficient pressure to allow the teeth to slip between one another, and draw out the wool. Keep carding the wool in this way, until most of it has transferred to the right-hand carder.

3 To transfer the wool back to the left-hand carder, brush the right-hand carder from the base to the handle, over to the left, then up from the handle to the base. Continue brushing out the wool in this way. To take the fleece off the carders, bring the handle end of the right-hand carder up the left-hand carder. As the fibres begin to lift, pull the right-hand carder away.

Drum carding

1 Feed the teased wool evenly onto the tray, and turn the handle clockwise. The wool will automatically feed in. Keep adding more wool until the teeth are full, then continue to turn the handle until all the fibres are parallel. When all the wool is smooth, find the point on the large drum where there is a break in the carding cloth. Insert a knitting needle under the wool at this gap, and gently lift up the fleece. Tear or cut the fleece where it has been lifted. Turn the handle anticlockwise to lift the fleece off the large drum.

FLAT FELT

The central core of each fibre of wool is covered in tiny scales. When the fibre is cool, the scales lie flat against each other, but hot water will lift them, causing the scales to become barbed like an open fir cone. Soap dissolved in the water acts as a catalyst in the process, increasing the movement of the fibres and breaking down the outer cortex of the core, making it react like a coiled spring. The friction and pressure of the felting process makes the fibres move backward, or towards their root, until each fibre has become so entangled it can move no further. This accounts for the shrinkage of the fibre during felting. When the scales are cool and dry, the tangled fibres are locked even more securely.

1 It is not essential to use a tray to make flat felt, but it will contain any excess water, and will protect the felt if it has to be moved or left at any stage. If you are using a tray, line it with a piece of clean cloth before you start to lay out the first pattern of felt. ▶

2 Different patterns can be laid on both faces of felt. For the pattern that is laid down first, you must remember to lay down the detail before the background. Lay the pattern onto the lining fabric, tearing out pieces of wool to the pattern required. This enables you to "sketch" with the wool.

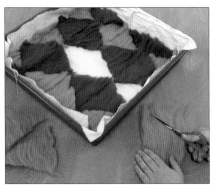

3 Shapes and patterns can be cut out from carded batts or teased-out sliver. Alternatively, the wool can be pulled out into thin wisps to give soft, blended edges and layers of colour.

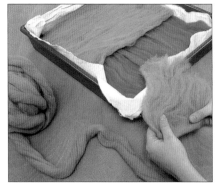

4 When the first pattern has been laid out, the background colour is put over the top. The wool must be carded, or teased out from carded slivers so that the fibres run in the same direction. This is not important for the pattern but must be done for the background, if the felting process is to be successful. If the first layer of wool is laid out so the fibres run from top to bottom of the tray, the second layer must be placed at right angles to this, so the fibres run from side to side.

5 Use at least three layers of carded wool to make the felt, each layer at right angles to the last, to ensure a strong and even fabric. Keep the layers thin if you want thin felt; keep adding layers for a thicker fabric. Patch up any thin or uneven layers with extra wool. The quality of the felt is determined by how carefully the fleece has been laid out and the evenness of the layers.

6 A second pattern may be laid out on the final layer of fleece. Dissolve one or two handfuls of soap flakes in a jug of hot water, using slightly more soap than you would use to wash a jumper.

7 The wool must be soaked with the hot soapy water but if it is poured in too quickly the fibres will part and holes may form. One option is to sprinkle water onto the wool with your hand. The water can also be dribbled onto the wool, in a spiralling motion. This is a good method for "tacking" the pattern in place. The water can also be poured over the back of your hand, allowing it to "fan out". This method is quicker than sprinkling, but be careful with the amount of water you pour on, as too much will cause the wool to float away.

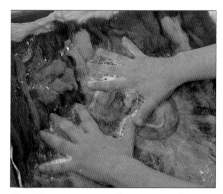

8 After pouring on the water with one of the above methods, press the water into the wool with the palms of your hands, and flatten the layers. Make sure the pattern has not moved too much, but if it has, move it back to the desired position. At this stage, details in the top pattern may be altered, or wool may be added or taken away.

9 Start the felting process very gently, by rubbing the surface with your hands in a circular movement. If the wool sticks to your hands, you will need to add more soap. This can be done by rubbing soap into your hands, or adding more directly to the wool. Rub the wool until it has "set" or until the fibres begin to lock together, even though there is no strength to the fabric.

10 The next stage is known as hardening the felt. Turn the edges of the lining fabric over the fleece. This will help keep the edges straight and firm. Place a rolling pin at one end of the tray, and roll up the fabric with the fleece.

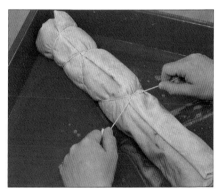

11 Fold a long piece of string in half, make a slip knot and pull it tight over one end of the roll. Criss-cross the two loose ends down the length of the roll, and tie with string at the other end firmly, so that the roll bulges out between the crossed pieces of string. Roll the bundle backwards and forwards on the tray, or on a ridged surface such as a draining board. Keep your hands moving along the length of the roll, to keep an even pressure.

12 When the string becomes loose, unwind the roll and carefully lift the felt away from the cloth. Use the flat of your hand to pull the fibres away from the cloth. Turn the felt 90 degrees, smooth it out with the flat of your hands, then roll up in the cloth again. Tie and roll the bundle back and forth as before. Repeat this process until the felt has been rolled in every direction, and on both sides. The felt will then have shrunk, and become a firm piece of fabric. Remove the cloth and rinse the felt under hot and cold running water until all traces of soap have been removed. The alternate hot and cold water also helps the final stage of the felting, which is known as fulling or milling. As an alternative to the lining cloth, a bamboo mat can be used to roll the felt. Bamboo mats are particularly useful for rolling large pieces of felt. ▶

FELT BALLS

A small felt ball is a good project to start with. It uses a small amount of fleece, so is easy to handle, but will allow you to experience the feel of the wool fibres changing into felt. A ball will probably take about 20–30 minutes to complete.

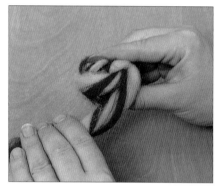

1 Twist the wool into a tight ball. If the finished ball is to be cut in half, use several colours.

2 Cover the ball in another layer of carded wool, wrapping it around smoothly and evenly. Keep the ball in your hand to stop it falling apart.

3 Dip the ball in hot, soapy water, squeezing it in your hand to wet it through to the middle.

4 Roll the ball very gently in your hand to begin the hardening process. Keep your hands cupped to retain the shape of the ball. As the fibres begin to mat together, steadily increase the pressure of your hands to move the fibres inside the ball. Dip the ball back in the water from time to time, to keep it warm and soapy. When the wool has fully felted, the ball will have shrunk considerably and will bounce if thrown hard on the table top. Rinse all the soap out of the ball and leave to dry. This will take quite a long time, but it may be put in a spin drier, or left on a radiator to speed up the process.

5 To make beads of different shapes, make a round ball as before, but felt only until the outer layer has hardened, and the inner core is still soft. You can then squeeze the ball into any shape that you like.

6 Roll the shaped bead in your hands, increasing the pressure steadily without losing the shape. Rinse and dry the bead as you would the ball.

POCKETS AND RESISTS

Three-dimensional, seamless shapes with pockets and flaps can be made in felt. This is done by using a resist – basically any material that will not felt – to separate two areas of fleece in the felting process. The technique is a little more complicated than flat felt.

1 These instructions are for a pocket, sealed on three sides and open at the top. Tease out the wool and lay out the first layer so that it is wider than the cloth resist. Put the second layer on the first; it must be longer than the first layer and the resist on one end. The third layer should be the same size as the resist. Alternate the direction of the fibres on all layers.

2 Pour hot, soapy water over the resist cloth and press it down to ensure that the fibres underneath are wet, but keep the edges dry. Fold the extra wool from the first and second layers over onto the cloth resist. Press the edges down onto the wet cloth to hold them in place.

3 Prepare two more layers of wool, the same sizes as the second and third layers. Lay them on the resist cloth and hold them in place with a little water.

4 Turn the whole bundle over, and put it on top of a final layer of wool, wider than the resist. (The cloth resist will now be in the middle of six layers of wool, with three on either side.)

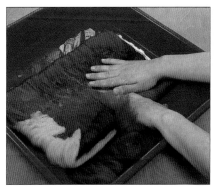

5 Fold the edges of the final layer of the bundle. Add more hot water and soap, and begin the felting process, first using your hands, then a rolling pin. Turn the felt over frequently, and roll in all directions to harden the felt evenly.

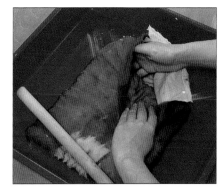

6 When the felt has become hard enough to handle more roughly, pull out the cloth resist. Put your hand inside the pocket to felt the inside and the edges. Continue to roll and pummel the felt until it has shrunk and become firm. Finish the pocket as for a flat piece of felt.

TEA COSY

THE INSULATING PROPERTIES OF FELT ENSURE THAT THE TEA COSY SHOWN HERE IS AS EFFECTIVE AT KEEPING A TEAPOT WARM AS IT IS DECORATIVE. THE FELT HAS A DIFFERENT PATTERN ON EACH SIDE OF THE FABRIC SO THE COSY IS REVERSIBLE. ALTERNATIVELY, YOU COULD TREAT THIS FELT PROJECT AS A "SAMPLER" AND EXPERIMENT FURTHER WITH YOUR OWN PATTERNS AND COLOUR COMBINATIONS TO DESIGN YOUR OWN WORK.

1 To make the spots for the inside of the felt, first pull out thin strips of purple fleece. Wrap each one round your fingertip, then roll it off with your thumb. Place each ring in the tray and fill the centres with a small ball of yellow fleece. Arrange the spots evenly all across the bottom of the tray.

2 Reserving 75 g (3 oz) of the fleece for the base, lay three layers of fabric in the tray over the arranged spots, with the fibres at right angles to the previous layer. The middle layer will show on the cut edge of the finished tea cosy.

3 Build up the outer pattern with thin strips of fleece. First lay a criss-cross grid in purple fleece. Then lay strips of blue fleece diagonally across the grid. Finally, lay strips of red fleece at right angles to the blue. Make the felt following the instructions in the Basic Techniques, taking care not to disturb the pattern when pouring on the hot water.

4 Lay a pattern of felt in a bowl for the base of the cosy. You can make patterns for both sides. When making the layers, keep each layer at 90 degrees to the previous one. Make the felt as before.

5 Trace the diagrams for the two sides and base of the cosy from the back of the book onto paper, enlarging them to size, and cut out the shapes from the green felt. Sew the two sides together, up to where the spout and handle will be, using ladder stitch, then stitch in the base.

6 The tea cosy is closed over the teapot using elasticated ribbon. Fold the ribbon in half lengthways and sew it along the seam. Then thread the elastic through, sewing the two ends together to form a circle.

MATERIALS AND EQUIPMENT YOU WILL NEED

300 G (11 OZ) FLEECE IN CARDED SLIVERS, THREE TYPES OF GREEN FOR THE COSY, PLUS PURPLE, YELLOW, BLUE AND RED FOR DECORATION • TRAY, APPROXIMATELY 45 CM (18 IN) SQUARE • SOAP FLAKES • BOWL WITH 16 CM (6¼ IN) DIAMETER FLAT BASE • PAPER AND PENCIL • SCISSORS • NEEDLE AND MATCHING SEWING THREAD • RIBBON, 30 x 2.5 CM (12 X 1 IN) • ELASTIC, 25 CM X 5 MM (10 X ¼ IN)

CUSHION COVER

BRIGHTEN UP THE DARK CORNERS OF AN ARMCHAIR WITH SOME UNUSUAL CUSHIONS. THE FLAPS OF THE FEATHER PATTERN ON THIS COVER ARE AN INTEGRAL PART OF THE FELT AND THE FIBRES HAVE BEEN BLENDED TOGETHER TO GIVE A GLOW OF COLOUR. EXPERIMENT WITH DIFFERENT COLOUR COMBINATIONS AND PATTERNS TO CREATE A CO-ORDINATED SET. YOU COULD SUBSTITUTE OTHER DESIGNS SUCH AS A SCALLOPED OR FRINGED EDGING.

1 For the felt make two layers of fleece each 45 cm (18 in) square and lay them in the tray.

3 Cut the calico into 5 strips, approximately 55 x 11 cm (22 x 4 ¼ in) Cover the three layers with a calico strip.

5 Make a third layer with two colours; this is the top of the first flap.

2 Hold two colours of carded sliver together and pull out the fibres. Lay the wool in the bottom quarter of the tray at 90 degrees to the previous layer of fleece.

4 Cover the calico with two more layers of fleece. The first needs to be twice the length of the calico, the second is not so long as the first one.

6 Lay a second strip of calico, the same dimensions as before, so that it slightly overlaps the first. ▶

MATERIALS AND EQUIPMENT YOU WILL NEED

150 G (6 OZ) FLEECE IN CARDED SLIVERS, VARIOUS COLOURS • TRAY, APPROXIMATELY 45 CM (18 IN) SQUARE • CALICO CLOTH 55 x 55 CM (22 x 22 IN) • SOAP FLAKES • ROLLING PIN • IRON • TAILOR'S CHALK • SCISSORS • NEEDLE AND MATCHING SEWING THREAD • WOOL FABRIC 50 CM (20 IN) • DRESSMAKER'S PINS • TACKING THREAD • CUSHION PAD

7 Repeat steps 4, 5 and 6 three more times until four flaps have been laid out on the tray.

8 Wet the fleece and make the felt following the instructions in the Basic Techniques but use a rolling pin to make the felt instead of wrapping it in calico.

9 When the wool has felted, but before it is fully finished, pull out the calico resists and then harden or finish the felt.

10 Press the finished felt with a hot iron to get a good smooth surface. Mark out the triangles with tailor's chalk then cut them out.

11 Turn the cut-out pieces round and slip them back underneath the flaps in the spaces, putting the triangles from the bottom row in the top row, those from the top row in the second row and so on. Sew the cut-outs in place, stitching along their top edges.

12 Cut the woollen fabric into two widths and turn the edges under. Pin and tack the wool to the felt, wrong sides together, so that the wool pieces overlap at the middle. Stitch the fabric to the felt round the edge. Insert the cushion pad through the split between the two halves of the fabric.

BOWL

USING A CHILD'S PLASTIC BALL AS A MOULD, THIS CHARMING BOWL IS PLEAS-INGLY SIMPLE TO MAKE. ALTHOUGH THE RESULT IS THREE-DIMENSIONAL, THE FELTING PROCESS IS EVEN EASIER THAN FOR A FLAT PIECE OF FABRIC. IF YOU ARE LUCKY YOU COULD END UP WITH TWO MATCHING BOWLS, AND ONCE YOU HAVE MASTERED THE TECHNIQUE IT COULD BE A SPRINGBOARD FOR OTHER EXCITING IDEAS AND PROJECTS.

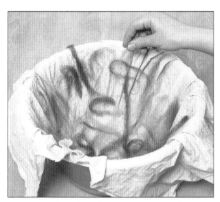

1 Line a bowl with a large piece of calico; it will need to cover the ball later (see step 5). Dampen the cloth with water to prevent the fleece from moving about. To make the pattern for the outside of the bowl, arrange wisps of coloured fleece over the dampened calico.

2 Place strips of carded sliver evenly over the pattern, overlapping them and using extra fleece at the bottom of the bowl. Make several layers in different colours and make sure there is sufficient excess to wrap over the ball later.

3 Make a roll of wool and use it to line the side of the bowl, positioning it parallel with the rim.

4 Drop the ball into the bowl, making sure there is sufficient fleece all round to cover it.

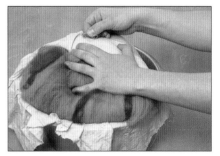

5 Draw the fleece up over the ball to cover it entirely. Draw up the calico over the wool and hold it in place with safety pins. ▶

MATERIALS AND EQUIPMENT YOU WILL NEED

BOWL, JUST LARGER THAN THE BALL• CALICO CLOTH, LARGE ENOUGH TO COVER THE BALL • FLEECE IN CARDED SLIVERS, VARIOUS COLOURS • CHILD'S PLASTIC BALL • SAFETY PINS • 2 ELASTICATED BANDAGES • SOAP FLAKES • TOWEL (OPTIONAL) • TAILOR'S CHALK • CRAFT KNIFE • SCISSORS

6 Remove the fabric-covered ball from the bowl and wrap the bandages tightly around it to hold it in a good round shape. The bandages will tighten round the ball as the felt shrinks. Secure the bandages with safety pins.

7 Dip the ball in a bowl of very hot, soapy water, turning the ball until it is thoroughly soaked. Place the ball in the washing machine and set on a long, hot cycle. An old towel in the washing machine with the ball will increase the amount of friction the ball receives.

8 Unwind the bandages in order to assess how well the wool has felted. If it has not felted enough, either put it though another machine-wash cycle or finish the job by hand. Unless the felt is still very soft, it is probably unnecessary to re-wrap the fabric.

9 When the fabric is thoroughly felted and dry, mark a cutting line with tailor's chalk. A thin patch or an unpleasing pattern may help you decide where to make the cut.

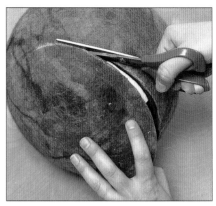

10 Start the cut with a sharp craft knife; this may puncture the ball. Continue the cut with a pair of sharp scissors. Remove the ball and trim the cut edge of the bowl if necessary.

APPLIQUÉD SCARF

MANY WOVEN FABRICS SUCH AS TWEED OR BAIZE ARE FULLED OR FELTED AS A FINISHING PROCESS TO MAKE A SMOOTH, FIRM FABRIC. THIS SCARF, DESIGNED BY FREDDIE ROBINS, USES FULLED FABRICS TO CREATE A WITTY DESIGN AND A RICH PATTERN OF TARTANS AND TWEEDS, WHICH ARE FURTHER EMBELLISHED WITH BUTTONS AND SHELLS. IF YOU WANT TO USE A WOOL FABRIC THAT HAS NOT BEEN FULLED AND FRAYS A LOT, WASH IT IN A SOLUTION OF HOT WATER AND SOAP FLAKES TO SHRINK AND FELT IT. WOOL CAN SHRINK BY AS MUCH AS 30% SO ALLOW FOR THIS WHEN YOU MAKE THE SCARF.

1 Draw the designs for the motifs onto paper and cut them out. Place each template on a different piece of fabric, draw round it with tailor's chalk and then cut out the shape.

3 Arrange the knitting wool on the scarf above the appliquéd pieces in the shape of a coat hanger and fix it in place with pins set at 90 degrees to the wool. Stitch the wool in position either by hand with a couching stitch or using a sewing machine set to a zigzag stitch.

4 Sew the buttons onto the appliquéd scarf using a sewing thread of a contrasting colour.

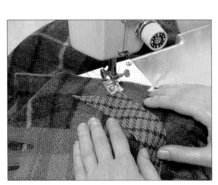

2 Pin the shapes to the scarf in a line right side up. Sew them in place with a zigzag stitch using a sewing machine.

5 Tie beads and shells to the hand motif using yarn of a contrasting colour and leaving the spare yarn as tassels. If you can find elongated buttons, sew these to the ends of the fingers as nails.

MATERIALS AND EQUIPMENT YOU WILL NEED

PAPER AND PENCIL • SCISSORS • TWEED AND TARTAN FABRIC SCRAPS • TAILOR'S CHALK • DRESSMAKER'S PINS • WOOL SCARF • SEWING MACHINE • THREAD AND YARN • LENGTH OF DOUBLE KNITTING WOOL • NEEDLE AND MATCHING AND CONTRASTING SEWING THREAD • BUTTONS • BEADS AND SHELLS

ACORN BUTTONS

THESE BEADED BUTTONS ARE IDEAL FOR COMPLEMENTING A KNITTED CARDI-GAN OR A SPECIAL JACKET, BUT THEY COULD ALSO BE USED IN OTHER WAYS. USE THEM AS WITTY AND EYE-CATCHING ORNAMENTS, OR THREAD THEM ON A LEATHER THONG, KNOTTED AT INTERVALS, TO MAKE A NECKLACE. THE AUTUMNAL COLOURS OF THE FELT AND THE MANY-FACETED GLASS BEADS MAKE THE ACORNS LOOK LIKE JEWELS.

1 Divide the brown and gold fleece into three and make each into three balls following the instructions in the Basic Techniques. For the brown fleece, keep rolling and felting the balls until they are very hard and bounce when dropped.

2 For the gold fleece, make into balls as before and when they are beginning to go hard, distort the balls into rugby balls with your fingers. Rinse all the balls thoroughly in water and allow to dry.

3 Cut each ball in half using a sharp craft knife. Cut across the narrow width of the gold rugby balls.

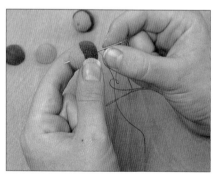

4 With their cut halves together, sew the half gold balls to the half brown balls using the button thread. Sew through the middle of each acorn and pull the thread tight to form a small dimple at the top of the gold ball.

5 Pull the thread through the brown ball and make three small loops, one on top of the other. Starting on your right, make a buttonhole shank.

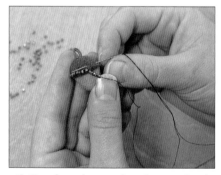

6 Use the polyester thread to sew beads round the rim of the acorn cup then spirally down to the shank to cover the cup. Sew the beads in groups of six: back-stitch three beads and catch down the thread before bringing the needle back out at the sixth bead.

MATERIALS AND EQUIPMENT YOU WILL NEED

6 G (¼ OZ) FLEECE, IN CORDED SLIVERS, BROWN AND GOLD • SOAP FLAKES • BOWL • CRAFT KNIFE • NEEDLE AND STRONG BUTTON THREAD • 1,000 SMALL FACETED GLASS BEADS • POLYESTER THREAD

APPLIQUÉD PURSE

Rich layers of differently coloured felt and stitching have been used by Teresa Searle to create this purse. The felt is made from pure wool knitting but old woollen knitwear felted in the washing machine could also be used. Bear in mind that yarn or a garment labelled "machine-washable" will not felt. How much material you need will depend on the size of the purse you want to make.

1 Use the template at the back of the book to make a paper pattern for the purse, enlarging it to size. Cut out the base pieces from the felted knitting and pin and tack them together. Sew on each appliqué piece with matching thread, using a sewing machine and a zigzag stitch or hand-sew the pieces with blanket stitch.

2 Build up the design, laying down four layers of fabric, pinning, tacking and sewing each one in place before starting the next layer. Trim off loose threads as you work.

3 Embroider on the detail by hand or use the sewing machine. Press the piece using a steam iron and pressing cloth. Measure the piece (it may have stretched) and cut a piece of lining to fit. Place the lining on the back of the felt. Pin and tack the edges of the purse and lining together. Cut the braid 2.5 cm (1 in) longer than the perimeter of the purse. With a 15 mm (1/2 in) seam allowance, sew the braid to make a circle and pin it on the felt side, 5 mm (1/4 in) from the edge. Straight-stitch the braid in position using the sewing machine, keeping just inside the edge. Trim away the excess fabric close to the edge of the braid. Fold the braid over the edge of the purse then pin, tack and sew it in place to the lining. Fold the bottom edge of the purse to two-thirds of the way up and pin in place. Over-sew the edges together on each side.

4 Tie a knot at each end of the cord and stitch in place inside each side seam of the purse. Locate the centre of the flap and sew on a button. Underneath, sew on the top half of a pop-fastener. Sew the other half of the pop-fastener to the centre of the bottom half of the purse, having made sure the two halves meet.

MATERIALS AND EQUIPMENT YOU WILL NEED
Paper and pencil • Scissors • Felted wool knitting (see Child's Cardigan) in several different colours • Dressmaker's pins • Tacking thread • Matching sewing thread • Sewing machine (optional) • Needles • Steam iron and pressing cloth • Lining fabric such as fine cotton or silk • Tape measure • Braid, 2.5 cm (1 in) wide • 140 cm (55 in) cord • Button • Pop-fastener

DOOR HANGING

THE INSPIRATION FOR THIS DOOR HANGING CAME FROM THE COLOURFUL, MIRRORED EMBROIDERIES OF GUJARAT IN INDIA. THE YELLOW BACKGROUND AND THE SUN MOTIF EXPLOIT THE EXHILARATING QUALITIES OF FELTMAKING AND, WHEN HUNG IN A DOORWAY, BOTH SIDES OF THE FELT CAN BE ENJOYED. A PIECE OF FELT IS MADE APPROXIMATELY 30% WIDER THAN THE DOOR FRAME AND CUT TO SHAPE LATER. FOR INSTANCE, FOR A DOOR MEASURING 76 CM (30 IN), 1 M (1 YD) OF FELT WAS LAID OUT. SCREW A CUP HOOK INTO EACH SIDE OF THE DOOR FRAME TO HANG THE CURTAIN POLE.

1 Lay out the first pattern onto a bamboo mat or calico cloth. Put down the detail before the main blocks of colour.

2 Put down three layers of teased-out carded sliver over the pattern. Here, the first and third layers are yellow, and the middle, red layer gives the yellow a warmer hue.

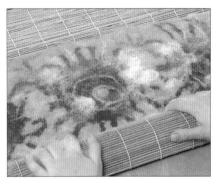

4 Make the felt following the instructions in the Basic Techniques.

3 Make the pattern for the top of the felt, dividing the bottom third of the rectangle into five petal shapes.

5 Rinse the finished felt then press it dry on both sides with a hot iron. This also gives the felt a good, smooth finish. ▶

MATERIALS AND EQUIPMENT YOU WILL NEED

350 G (12 OZ) FLEECE IN CARDED SLIVERS, VARIOUS COLOURS • BAMBOO MAT OR CALICO CLOTH • SCISSORS • SOAP FLAKES • IRON • SEWING MACHINE • CONTRASTING SEWING THREADS • CONTRASTING EMBROIDERY THREADS • KNITTING WOOL • NEEDLE • CURTAIN POLE • CUP HOOKS

6 Cut away the excess felt from around the petal shapes and trim the other sides of the felt if necessary.

7 Using a sewing machine, stich round the edge with a small straight stitch using a contrasting sewing thread to give a finished appearance.

8 Use the knitting wool to make five buttonhole loops along the top of the hanging for a hanging pole.

9 Make five large balls following the instructions in the Basic Techniques. Make simple tassels from embroidery thread and sew one onto each ball.

10 Sew one ball and tassel onto the end of each petal with embroidery thread. Pass a curtain pole through the loops at the top of the hanging and hang from cup hooks.

THROW

THE FELTMAKING PROCEDURE FOR THIS PROJECT IS EASY. THE EMBROIDERED CLOTH IS SIMPLY PUT INTO THE WASHING MACHINE WITH TOO MUCH SOAP AND SET ON A HOT CYCLE — EVERYTHING YOU WISH YOU HAD NEVER DONE TO YOUR FAVOURITE JUMPER. THE FELTING ACTION SHRINKS THE FABRIC AND EMBROIDERY TOGETHER TO GIVE THE APPEARANCE OF AN EMBOSSED BLANKET. THE FINISHED RESULT IS DECEPTIVELY SOPHISTICATED.

1 Lay the wool suiting fabric flat on the floor or on a large table. Following the diagram at the back of the book as a guide, mark out the pattern for the stitchwork on the fabric using tailor's chalk.

2 Tack over the tailor's chalk in large stitches using a tacking thread in a contrasting colour.

3 On the border, follow the tacking stitches with a running stitch using the double knitting wool. Remove the tacking stitches at the end of each section.

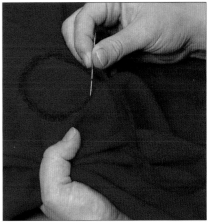

4 For each circle, start on the outer edge and work a spiral into the centre in running stitch. ▶

MATERIALS AND EQUIPMENT YOU WILL NEED
150 x 150 CM (59 x 59 IN) WOOL SUITING FABRIC • TAILOR'S CHALK • NEEDLE • TACKING THREAD • 115 G (4 OZ) DOUBLE KNITTING WOOL •
SOAP FLAKES • WASHING MACHINE OR WASHBOARD • SCISSORS • STEAM IRON

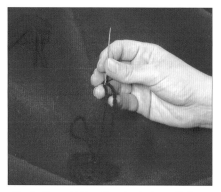

5 In the middle of each circle pull the yarn that is left on the needle up to the top of the fabric. Make a 7.5 cm (3 in) loop and and take the yarn back through the fabric then back up to the top again.

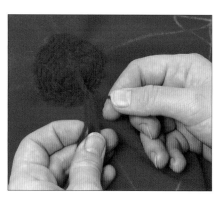

6 Remove the needle and cut the loop. Plait the three strands together.

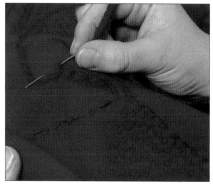

7 Follow the diagram at the back of the book to embroider the border patterns. Work these designs in simple running stitch and chain stitch. Keep the stitches small and even for the best effect.

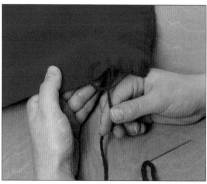

8 Finish the raw edges of the throw with blanket stitch.

9 Check that all loose ends are secure and that the plaits have not come undone but do not cut anything off until after the felting process. Place the fabric in the washing machine, with plenty of soap on a short, hot cycle. Alternatively, felt it by hand in the sink using hot soapy water and an old-fashioned washboard. When the cycle has finished, remove the felt and pull it back into shape. Pull the plaited strands straight while still damp. Pull off any loose wool that has been left.

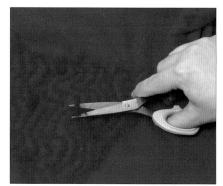

10 Snip off any untidy bits on the back of the throw. While the throw is still damp, use a hot steam iron to open out the stitches where they have shrunk and buckled up the fabric. Do not use the weight of the iron on the stitches as it will flatten them.

NECKLACE

THIS BRIGHTLY COLOURED NECKLACE IS FUN TO WEAR AND EASY TO MAKE. THE LARGE BEADS ARE VERY LIGHT AND WILL NOT WEIGH YOU DOWN. YOU CAN USE UP SCRAPS OF FLEECE FROM OTHER PROJECTS TO MAKE UP THE BEADS. EXPERIMENT WITH DIFFERENT SIZES AND SHAPES OF BEADS, AND HAVE FUN MIXING COLOURS TO CREATE A MARBLED EFFECT. USE THE SAME TECHNIQUE TO MAKE A MATCHING BRACELET.

1 Divide the fleece into bundles to make 19–21 beads, each containing two or three colours. Wind and twist each bundle into a tight ball.

2 To make the balls into hard beads follow the instructions in the Basic Techniques. A good test for hardness is to throw a bead down; if it bounces once or twice it is hard. Rinse each bead under a hot tap then a cold one and allow to dry. (A spin dryer will help speed up the drying process.)

3 Lay the beads out in the order you want them to be threaded. Thread a crimp bead onto the nylon-coated wire and then one half of the clasp. Turn the wire back through the crimp bead and crush the bead using a small pair of pliers to secure the wire.

4 Thread the wire onto a large needle then push this through the beads and thread them onto the wire. Attach the other half of the necklace clasp as described in step 3.

MATERIALS AND EQUIPMENT YOU WILL NEED
50 G (2 OZ) FLEECE, IN CARDED SLIVERS, VARIOUS COLOURS • SOAP FLAKES • 2 CRIMP BEADS • NYLON-COATED JEWELLERY WIRE • NECKLACE CLASP • SMALL PLIERS • LARGE NEEDLE

EARRINGS

A FELT BALL CUT IN HALF TO REVEAL AN INTRICATE PATTERN OF COLOURS MAKES A DELIGHTFUL PAIR OF EARRINGS. THE EXCITEMENT THAT COMES WITH CUTTING THROUGH THE BALL TO SEE WHAT THE PATTERN WILL BE LIKE WILL PROBABLY PROMPT YOU TO MAKE MORE THAN ONE PAIR. OTHER HALF-BALLS CAN BE USED TO MAKE BUTTONS OR BROOCHES, OR CAN BE CLUSTERED TOGETHER TO MAKE LARGER PIECES.

1 Make a ball by twisting and wrapping two or more colours of fleece together. The more twists, turns and colours you use in the middle of the ball, the more intricate the resulting pattern will be. Make the ball into felt following the instructions in the Basic Techniques. Ensure the ball is felted all the way through and is very firm. Allow to dry.

2 When the ball is completely dry, cut it in half using a craft knife. The pattern should stay in place; if the ball is not felted all the way through, the middle will bulge out at this point.

3 To make the felt really hard, you can dip it in felteen hat stiffener. The felt must be absolutely dry as water reacts with the stiffener and will make a cloudy white film on the surface. An alternative is to dip the felt in PVA glue diluted with water, although this leaves a shiny surface.

4 Mix a two-part epoxy resin according to the manufacturer's instructions and use it to fix the earring backs or findings to the backs of the earrings.

MATERIALS AND EQUIPMENT YOU WILL NEED

5 G (1/8 OZ) FLEECE, IN CARDED SLIVERS, VARIOUS COLOURS • SOAP FLAKES • TRIMMING OR CRAFT KNIFE •
FELTEEN HAT STIFFENER OR PVA GLUE • 2-PART EPOXY RESIN • EARRING BACKS OR FINDINGS

BRACELET

THIS CHUNKY BRACELET IS DECEPTIVELY LIGHT AND SOFT TO WEAR. YOU CAN VARY THE END RESULT BY EMBROIDERING A FINISHED BRACELET, SEWING ON BEADS OR ARTIFICIAL FLOWERS OR INCORPORATING OTHER TYPES OF YARN AS YOU MAKE IT UP. SELECT YOUR COLOURS CAREFULLY, AND ENJOY BLENDING THEM TO MAKE A WONDERFUL MARBLED FINISH. WEAR THE BRACELET WITH THE EARRINGS IN CO-ORDINATING COLOURS.

1 Divide each length of fleece in half. Make them up into two plaits, leaving two leftover strands. Tie the two plaits and the two strands together at one end with string attached to a heavy weight. Twist the plaits and strands tightly together and tie them securely with string. Wet the wool thoroughly with hot, soapy water, keeping the plaits and strands in a twist.

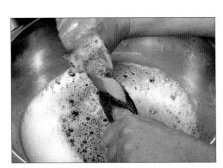

2 Rub the length of the fibres with plenty of soap, keeping the twist pulled taut against the weight with one hand. The fibres will soon felt together, after which they will not unwind.

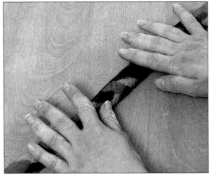

3 When the wool has felted on the outside, remove the weight and roll the "sausage" firmly on the worktop to felt the fibres in the middle.

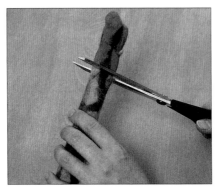

4 While the sausage is still flexible, cut off the ends tied with string. Wrap it round your wrist to check the fit and that it will go over your hand when joined up. Trim down as required.

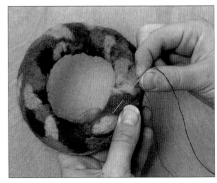

5 Stitch the two ends together using a needle and thread. Take the thread from end to end, inside the felt, to make the join strong.

6 Felt the bracelet again in hot water and soap to shrink the inside curve and to hide the stitched join. Rinse and allow to dry.

MATERIALS AND EQUIPMENT YOU WILL NEED

40 G (1½ OZ) FLEECE IN THREE COLOURS • STRING • HEAVY WEIGHT • SOAP FLAKES • SCISSORS • NEEDLE AND MATCHING SEWING THREAD

MOBILE

ENCRUSTED WITH GLASS BEADS AND PINS, THE STARS AND PLANETS OF THIS MOBILE LITERALLY SHINE AND SPARKLE. YOU CAN UNWIND AND RELAX WHILE WATCHING THE HEAVENLY BODIES FLOATING ABOVE. BY CHANGING THE COLOURS,

YOU COULD TURN THE COMPONENTS INTO FESTIVE TREE DECORATIONS. TO FIX THE PINS PERMANENTLY IN THE FELT, DIP THE SHARP END IN STRONG ADHESIVE JUST BEFORE PRESSING THEM INTO THE FELT.

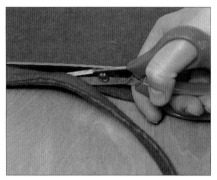

1 Cut a long, thin strip of felt from the sheet of hand-rolled felt.

2 Roll the strip into a Catherine wheel and stitch it to hold it together.

4 Thread two beads and a sequin onto some pins, dip the points in adhesive and push them immediately into a large felt ball, spacing them evenly.

3 Thread some small glass beads onto some pins, all in the same order, and push the pins, dipped in adhesive and evenly spaced, into the felt around the edge of the Catherine wheel.

MATERIALS AND EQUIPMENT YOU WILL NEED
30 x 12 CM (12 x 5 IN) SHEET OF HAND-ROLLED FELT, WITH CONTRASTING COLOUR SANDWICHED IN MIDDLE (SEE BASIC TECHNIQUES) •
SCISSORS • NEEDLE • THREAD • SELECTION OF SMALL GLASS BEADS OF DIFFERENT SHAPES AND SIZES • DRESSMAKER'S PINS • STRONG ADHESIVE •
SEQUINS • FELT BALLS, 3 LARGE, 6 SMALL • BUGLE BEADS • TAILOR'S CHALK • SILVER METALLIC THREAD •
2 x 25 CM (10 IN) LENGTHS OF MEDIUM WIRE

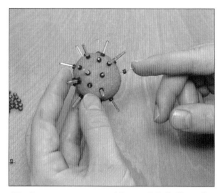

5 Decorate a second large felt ball with a different arrangement of beads. Here, single round beads on pins have been alternated with a combination of a round bead and a bugle bead on pins.

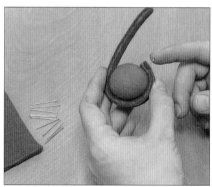

6 Encircle the third large felt ball with a halo cut from a narrow strip from the felt sheet. Pin one end to the ball.

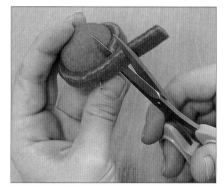

7 Wrap the strip round the ball and cut off the excess.

8 Gently press pins at regular intervals around the halo. Roll the ball along the worktop to push the pins in firmly.

9 Draw two stars on a piece of flat felt using tailor's chalk. Cut them out.

10 Make five tassels for each star. First wrap silver metallic thread loosely but evenly round two fingers approximately 20–30 times. ▶

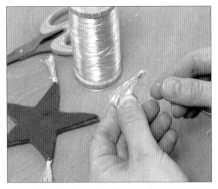

11 Slip the thread off your fingers and bind one end of the loop with the metallic thread, securing it with several stitches. Cut off the other end to complete the tassle.

13 Thread the stars and the planets onto the metallic thread. Tie a couple of small beads at the end of each piece of thread to prevent it from pulling through the felt.

15 Tie the stars and planets to the medium wires with their threads. Hang the mobile up to adjust the balance of the wires, then fix everything in position with dabs of adhesive.

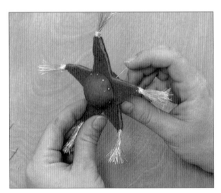

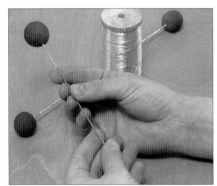

12 Cut two small felt balls in half and pin one half on either side of each star.

14 Wrap metallic thread round the wire to cover it. Apply adhesive to the ends of the two lengths of wire and push a small felt ball onto each end.

BROOCH

FELT FLOWER BROOCHES WERE POPULAR IN THE 1930S AND 1940S, WHEN THE BOLD SHAPES AND COLOURS OF FELT PROVIDED A LIVELY COMPLEMENT TO A DULL WINTER COAT OR PLAIN HAT. REMINISCENT OF THOSE EARLIER DESIGNS, THIS BROOCH USES A THINNER COMMERCIAL FELT THAN WOULD HAVE BEEN AVAILABLE THEN. AND THE CHOICE OF COLOURS TODAY IS FAR GREATER THAN BEFORE, SO EXPERIMENT WITH ALL THE POSSIBLE COLOUR COMBINATIONS.

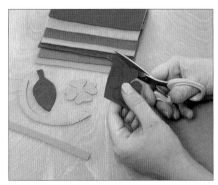

1 Trace the templates from the back of the book and enlarge them to size. Transfer to the felt and cut out the pieces.

3 Stitch the flower centres in place. Pinch the backs of the petals, and stitch to give them more shape.

5 Using a sewing machine, satin-stitch along the length of each leaf to make a rib. Sew the four leaves together in a fan shape. Fold the stalks in half and sew them to the leaves. Then sew the flowers to the leaves over the fold of the stalks.

2 Put the petals together in contrasting pairs. Cut a fringed edge along a strip of the yellow felt for the flower centres. Roll them up and place them in the centre of the petal pairs.

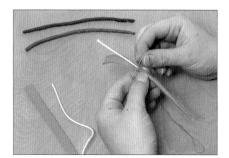

4 Cut the string into three 15 cm (6 in) lengths, then sew each into a strip of green felt to create the stalks.

6 Turn the brooch over and stitch on the brooch back.

MATERIALS AND EQUIPMENT YOU WILL NEED
PAPER AND PENCIL • 10 x 5 CM (4 x 2 IN) COMMERCIAL FELT PIECES, ONE EACH OF PINK, MAUVE AND ORANGE •
14.5 x 3 CM (5¾ x 1¼ IN) FELT PIECES, ONE EACH OF YELLOW AND THREE SHADES OF GREEN • SCISSORS •
NEEDLE AND MATCHING SEWING THREAD • 42 CM (16½ IN) STRING • SEWING MACHINE • BROOCH BACK

BATH MAT

HAND-ROLLED FELT CARPETS DO NOT USUALLY STAND UP TO THE WEAR AND TEAR OF OUTDOOR SHOES BUT THEY DO MAKE IDEAL MATS FOR THE BATHROOM WHERE WET FEET WILL FELT THEM UP A LITTLE BIT MORE EACH TIME THE MAT IS USED. THE FELT CARPETS OF CENTRAL ASIA ALWAYS HAVE A PATTERN ON BOTH SIDES. WHILE THIS BATH MAT HAS A TRADITIONAL DESIGN ON THE UNDER-SIDE, THE TOP PATTERN IS MADE UP OF WOVEN FLEECE.

1 Arrange strands and pieces of fleece directly onto a bamboo mat or large piece of calico to make the pattern for the underside of the mat.

2 Tease out the carded fleece and put down two layers over the pattern, following the instructions in the Basic Techniques.

3 Lay down a third layer of fleece to form part of the top pattern and to form the fringe of the mat. Cut eight strips of the fleece slightly longer than the base layers and cut the other strips to the width of the base. The exact number required will depend on the size of your mat. Weave the strips together leaving a fringe at each end.

4 Place the woven layer on top of the base layers and make the felt, following the instructions in the Basic Techniques and rolling the fabric up in the bamboo mat or calico. Trim the finished felt if necessary.

MATERIALS AND EQUIPMENT YOU WILL NEED
225 G (8 OZ) FLEECE IN CARDED SLIVERS, VARIOUS COLOURS • BAMBOO MAT OR CALICO CLOTH • SOAP FLAKES • SCISSORS

CACTUS CURTAIN

Felt may not be the first fabric that springs to mind as a medium for machine embroidery but if the fabric is well prepared and care is taken, the results are stunning. The flatness of the felt makes a marvel-lous foil for the lustre of the threads and enhances the texture of the stitching. These contrasts are used to great effect in this curtain designed by Helen Banzhaf.

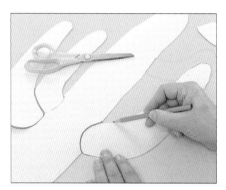

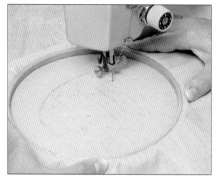

1 Trace the template from the back of the book, enlarging to the size required, and allowing an extra 8 cm (3 in) all round to allow for shrinkage during embroidery. Using a sharp pencil carefully draw the outlines of the cactus shapes on the fabric.

2 Transfer the vertical ribs and dots for the spines to the fabric as guides for the embroidery. They do not have to be exact. Pin vilene interfacing to the underside of each cactus to prevent the felt from stretching too much when it is embroidered. Working from the bottom of the cactus, place the pencilled shape tautly in the embroidery hoop. Prepare the sewing machine: remove the presser foot, select straight stitch, adjust the stitch length to 0, and drop the feed-dog.

3 On the right-hand cactus, stitch in the outline (edge and vertical ribs) with several lines of lime green thread. Then stitch the rows of dots in the same colour working spirally from the centre of each dot outwards. Remove the fabric from the hoop and cut the threads very close to the embroidery. ▶

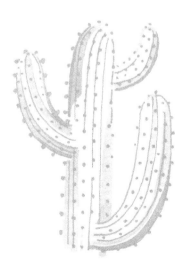

MATERIALS AND EQUIPMENT YOU WILL NEED

Paper and pencil • 1 x 1 m (1 x 1 yd) commercial felt • Scissors • Vilene interfacing • Embroidery hoop • Sewing machine • Machine embroidery threads in lime green, light gold, emerald green, chartreuse and dark gold • Steam iron • Tacking thread • Matching sewing thread • Wooden dowel

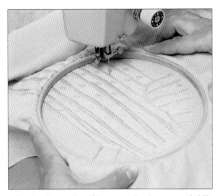

4 Replace the fabric in the hoop and fill in the background area between the dots and ribs. Outline the left side of the vertical ribs with light gold and then the right side with emerald green.

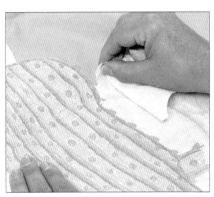

5 Tear the vilene interfacing away from the underside of the embroidery. Move the embroidery hoop up the cactus and continue embroidering the large cactus as described above.

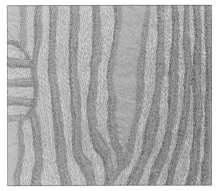

6 Embroider the smaller cactus in the same way but omitting the dots and changing the fill-in colour to chartreuse and the left highlighting to dark gold.

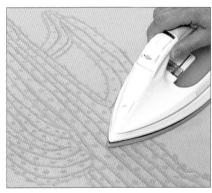

7 Press the embroidered felt very carefully with a steam iron, first on the wrong side, then on the right. It is best to press on a large flat surface as draping the felt over an ironing board will stretch it. Pin the pattern back onto the felt and trim it to the edge of the pattern.

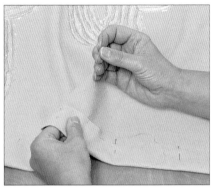

8 Turn and tack the casing at the top (to fit the dowel) and the hem at the bottom, then machine-stitch them in place.

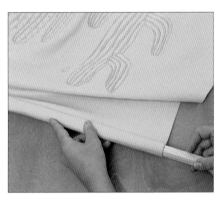

9 Insert the wooden dowel in the casing ready to hang the curtain.

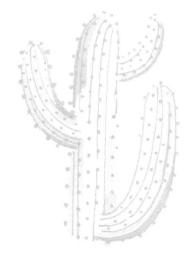

WALL HANGING

THE WALL HANGING DESIGNED AND MADE BY DAWN DUPREE WAS DEVELOPED FROM A PASTEL DRAWING. PAINTERLY EFFECTS IN THE FELT CAN BE ACHIEVED BY BLENDING TWO COLOURS OF FLEECE, EITHER BY HAND OR WITH A CARDER.

THE MOVEMENT OF FIBRES DURING THE FELTING PROCESS GIVES A LOVELY SPONTANEOUS FEEL TO THE DESIGN ON THE FELT. THIS IS A GREAT PROJECT FOR EXPERIMENTING WITH PATTERN-MAKING.

1 Tease out the carded sliver for the base layer and lay it flat. Place the second layer, in a different colour, with the fibres at 90 degrees to the first. Some of the fibres from these two layers will work up to the top layer of felt and influence the final colour effect.

2 Add a third layer in a third colour with its fibres running at 90 degrees to the second layer. This layer will be the background for the picture.

3 Cut out circles and rectangles from fleece that has been teased out. Manipulate these into figures and arrange them on the background layer.

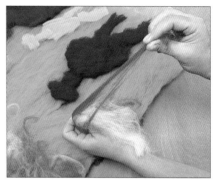

4 Blend two colours of fleece by hand and then lay them down on the background in swirls.

5 Pull out thin strips from the carded fleece and use it to make fine lines of detail in the design.

▶

MATERIALS AND EQUIPMENT YOU WILL NEED

200 G (7 OZ) FLEECE, IN CARDED SLIVERS, VARIOUS COLOURS • SCISSORS • SOAP FLAKES • STEAM IRON •
COTTON BRAID, 2 X THE WIDTH AND LENGTH OF THE HANGING • DRESSMAKER'S PINS • NEEDLE AND MATCHING SEWING THREAD •
VELCRO, THE WIDTH OF THE HANGING • PVA GLUE • THIN WOODEN BATTEN, THE WIDTH OF THE HANGING

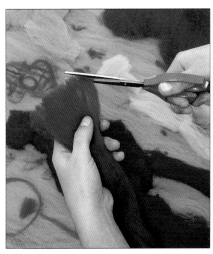

6 Cut off small pieces of carded fleece to make spots.

7 When you have laid out your pattern or picture, make up the felt following the instructions in the Basic Techniques.

8 After rinsing the felt, dry it with a hot iron, using the steam to press out any lumps or bumps in the felt. Iron it very carefully on both sides.

9 Trim off the rough edges and make the corners square. Fold the cotton braid in half lengthways, pin and stitch it around the edge of the hanging.

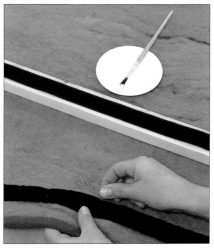

10 Stitch one half of the velcro to the back of the hanging, along the top edge. Glue the other half to a piece of wood. Then press both sides of the velcro together to attach the picture.

JUGGLING BALLS

A LARGE MARBLE IN THE CENTRE OF EACH OF THESE BALLS GIVES THEM BETTER WEIGHT FOR JUGGLING. THE BALLS CAN BE MADE TO ANY SIZE AND LARGE, UNWEIGHTED, BRIGHTLY COLOURED BALLS MAKE GREAT INDOOR TOYS FOR YOUNG CHILDREN, OR EVEN PETS. IF YOU HAVE THE PATIENCE TO MAKE HUNDREDS OF SMALL BALLS WITHOUT WEIGHTED CENTRES, YOU CAN HANG THEM ON STRONG THREAD TO MAKE A DOOR CURTAIN.

1 Tease out the carded fleece of the base colour. Place a marble at the end of the strip and wind the fleece firmly round it. Continue winding the fleece to form a ball about one-third larger than you want the finished ball to be.

2 Wrap two strands of knitting wool together round the fleece ball in a random pattern. It does not matter if the wool causes the fleece to indent.

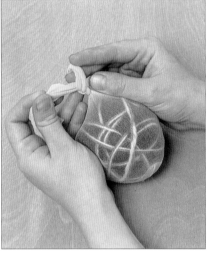

3 Place the ball in the toe of the tights or a stocking. Cut off the excess and tie the end in a firm knot. Dip the ball in hot, soapy water until it is thoroughly soaked. Place the ball in a washing machine and set it on a short, hot cycle. Several balls can be placed in the washing machine together.

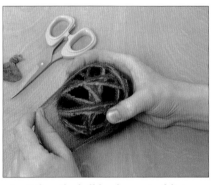

4 When the ball has begun to felt in the washing machine, remove it. Cut off the knot and pull off the stocking. If the ball has felted a lot, removing the stocking can be a slow, difficult job.

5 The ball may look rather fluffy. Dip it in very hot, soapy water then finish the felting process with your hands until the ball is the size and density you want. Rinse out all the soap under a tap, spin dry if possible and allow to dry.

MATERIALS AND EQUIPMENT YOU WILL NEED

50 G (2 OZ) FLEECE, IN CARDED SLIVERS, VARIOUS COLOURS • LARGE MARBLES • KNITTING WOOL • PAIR OF TIGHTS OR STOCKINGS •
SCISSORS • SOAP FLAKES • WASHING MACHINE • SPIN DRYER (OPTIONAL)

COLLAR

THE FELTING PROPERTIES OF WOOL ARE SUCH THAT WHEN ANY OTHER OPEN-WEAVE FABRIC, EVEN LACE, IS LAID ON TOP OF THE FLEECE IT WILL BECOME PART OF THE FELT. DURING THE FELTING PROCESS THE WOOL FIBRES MOVE OVER AND AROUND THE NON-WOOL FIBRES LOCKING THEM INTO THE FELT. THE LACY COLLAR SHOWN HERE HAS THE FEEL OF AN ELIZABETHAN RUFF. IT COULD BE WORN OVER A PLAIN WOOL SWEATER OR A WINTER COAT.

1 Place three very thin layers of fleece in the bottom of the tray, as described in the Basic Techniques.

2 Lay the lace on top of the fleece. Dampen the fleece and lace with hot, soapy water and start to make the felt gently with your hands following the instructions in the Basic Techniques, making sure the lace stays in place. Don't lift a corner to see how the felting is progressing as this would break off the fibres and spoil the collar.

3 When the felting is complete, rinse the felt, then press while still wet with a hot iron, pulling out the edges and stretching out the lace. Allow the felt to dry.

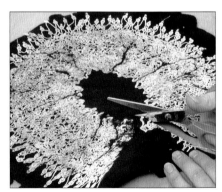

4 When the felt is dry, cut out the shape of the collar. Stitch buttons along one cut edge and make button loops along the other to fasten the collar.

MATERIALS AND EQUIPMENT YOU WILL NEED

50 G (2 OZ) FLEECE • TRAY • 1 M (1 YD) LACE • SOAP FLAKES • IRON • SCISSORS • BUTTONS • NEEDLE AND MATCHING SEWING THREAD

CHILD'S CARDIGAN

KNITTED FABRIC CAN BE THROWN INTO THE WASHING MACHINE AND PUT ON A LONG, HOT WASH TO BE TRANSFORMED INTO A FELT THAT RETAINS THE FLEXIBILITY OF KNITWEAR. IT CAN BE CUT WITHOUT FEAR OF UNRAVELLING AND USED TO MAKE UP WARM GARMENTS SUCH AS THIS CARDIGAN MADE BY KATIE MAWSON. THE APPEALING DESIGN IS SURE TO BE POPULAR WITH ALL AGES, AND THE BASIC TECHNIQUE CAN BE USED TO MAKE A CARDIGAN OF ANY SIZE. WHEN CHOOSING THE WOOL (SHETLAND IS EXCELLENT FOR THIS PURPOSE) BEAR IN MIND THAT ANY LABELLED "MACHINE-WASHABLE" WILL NOT FELT.

1 Knit a sample square in stocking stitch. Measure the piece accurately and record the measurement. Felt the piece in the washing machine, making a note of the wash cycle. Allow to dry.

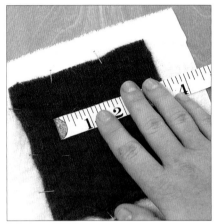

2 Measure the sample piece again and compare the measurement with the previous one to caculate how much the fabric has shrunk. Knit enough fabric to make the cardigan and appliqué details, allowing for shrinkage. The cardigan is made from one colour, and the appliqué details in contrasting colours. Felt the fabric in the washing machine using the same cycle as for the sample piece.

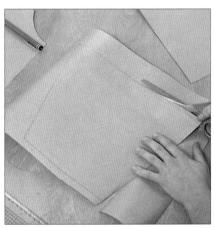

3 Trace the templates from the back of the book onto paper, enlarging to the size required, and cut out the pattern pieces for the cardigan.

MATERIALS AND EQUIPMENT YOU WILL NEED

200 G (7 OZ) DOUBLE KNITTING WOOL SUCH AS SHETLAND • SIZE 8 KNITTING NEEDLES • TAPE MEASURE • SOAP FLAKES • WASHING MACHINE • ODDMENTS OF DOUBLE KNITTING WOOL FOR THE APPLIQUÉ DETAIL • PAPER AND PENCIL • SCISSORS • DRESSMAKER'S PINS • DARNING NEEDLE • FINE WOOL FOR STITCHING • SEWING MACHINE • MATCHING SEWING THREAD • 5 BUTTONS • EMBROIDERY THREAD

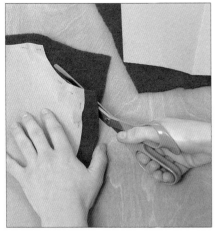

4 Pin the pattern pieces to the felted fabric and cut out the shapes.

6 Cut the buttonholes and finish them with buttonhole stitch using wool.

8 Pin the templates to the contrasting felted fabric.

5 Using wool of a contrasting colour and a darning needle, finish the raw edges of the cardigan with blanket stitch.

7 Trace the templates from the back of the book, enlarging them to size, and cut out the patterns for the appliqué shapes.

9 Cut out the appliqué shapes using small sharp scissors. Pin the appliqué shapes in position on the cardigan pieces. ▶

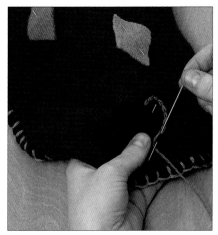

10 Chain-stitch the shapes in place using fine wool.

12 Sew the buttons onto the front of the cardigan.

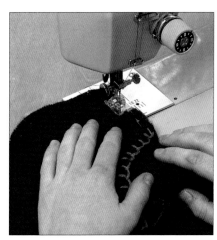

11 With right sides together, pin and then machine-stitch the cardigan pieces together.

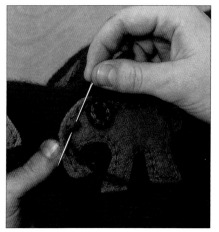

13 To finish, embroider the eye on the elephant.

CHILD'S SKIRT

BACK IN THE 1950S, FELT CIRCLE SKIRTS, OFTEN DECORATED WITH SCOTTY-DOG MOTIFS OR RIC-RAC BRAID, WERE A POPULAR FASHION "MUST-HAVE". THIS EXTRAVAGANTLY APPLIQUÉD SKIRT, DESIGNED BY CONSUELO MEJIA-BRUTON, HAS AN UNDERWATER THEME. AS COMMERCIAL FELT IS NOT MACHINE WASHABLE, THIS SKIRT IS BEST KEPT FOR PARTIES OR OTHER SPECIAL OCCASIONS. THE BASIC SKIRT DESIGN CAN BE SCALED UP TO FIT AN ADULT.

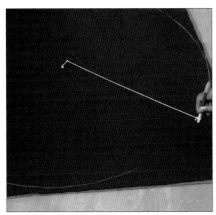

1 Lay the turquoise felt flat on a large board then lay the purple felt on top of it. Secure one end of the string to the centre of the felt using a pin pressed through the fabric into the board. Tie a fabric marker to the other end of the string, making the string about 50 cm (20 in), and use this as a compass to draw the circle for the skirt. Shorten the string and draw an inner circle to the required measurement for the waist.

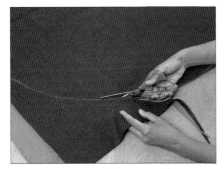

2 Cut the two circles out. At the waist, cut a 12.5 cm (5 in) long opening down the skirt.

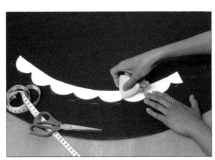

3 Make a paper template for the scalloped edge. Then mark out the scalloped edge, using the template and tailor's chalk, and cut along this line.

4 Trace the templates from the back of the book for the appliqué motifs, enlarging them to the size required, and cut out the shapes from some contrasting colours of felt. ▶

MATERIALS AND EQUIPMENT YOU WILL NEED

1 M (1 YD) COMMERCIAL FELT, TURQUOISE AND PURPLE PLUS SMALLER AMOUNTS IN SEVERAL COLOURS • LARGE BOARD • STRING • PANEL PIN • TAPE MEASURE • DRESSMAKER'S SCISSORS • PAPER AND PENCIL • TAILOR'S CHALK • NEEDLE AND METALLIC THREAD IN SEVERAL COLOURS • HOLE PUNCH • DRESSMAKER'S PINS • TACKING THREAD • SATIN BIAS BINDING, FOR THE WAIST BAND • SEWING MACHINE (OPTIONAL) • 120 X 1.5 CM (48 X ¾ IN) SATIN RIBBON • 2 M X 2.5 CM (2 YD X 1 IN) GREEN COMMERCIAL FELT

5 Embroider the heart motif onto the large fish motif using metallic thread.

6 Using a hole punch, make eye-holes on all of the fish, a speckled pattern on the smaller fish motif and spots on the starfish motifs.

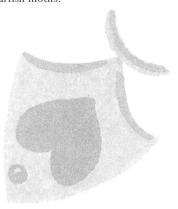

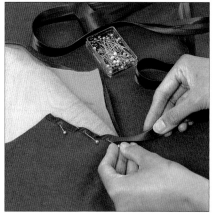

7 Pin and tack the satin bias binding to the two layers of felt at the waist, then stitch them in place either by hand or using a sewing machine.

8 Cut the edging in green felt for the hem of the skirt. Pin, tack and sew it in place. Pin the motifs around the skirt and tack them in position.

9 Sew the motifs onto the skirt using a variety of differently coloured metallic threads and bold stitches.

10 Using the hole punch, make five holes along each side of the back opening and lace up the skirt with the satin ribbon.

DOLL

Felt has always been a popular choice of fabric for toy-making. In addition to the wide choice of colours and the fact that it is available in small quantities, felt is easy to sew and needs no finishing. This cheeky doll by Isabel Stanley will please young and old alike. Once you have mastered the technique, you can adapt the basic pattern to make a whole family of dolls with different outfits.

1 Trace the templates from the back of book, enlarging them to the required size, and cut out pattern pieces for the parts of the doll. Cut out two head pieces from the flesh-coloured felt and mark the face on one of them. Embroider the features by hand.

2 Cut out the two hair pieces from the brown velvet and stitch on the front and back head pieces.

3 Cut out four leg pieces from the flesh-coloured felt, four sock pieces and four short pieces from the linen. Stitch one piece of linen to each end of the leg pieces, right sides together. Place each pair of leg pieces right sides together and stitch along the side seams. Turn through to the right side and stitch across the linen at the top of each leg.

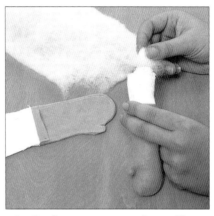

4 Cut four arm pieces and assemble as for the legs, attaching white linen to the tops of the arms only. Turn the arms through to the right side, stuff with wadding and stitch across the top edge. ▶

MATERIALS AND EQUIPMENT YOU WILL NEED

Paper and pencil • Scissors • 50 cm (20 in) commercial felt, flesh-coloured, plus smaller quantities in several colours • Needle and contrasting hand embroidery threads • Scraps of brown velvet • Scraps of white linen • Sewing machine • Matching sewing threads • Wadding • 15 cm x 5 mm (6 x ¼ in) ribbon • Buttons

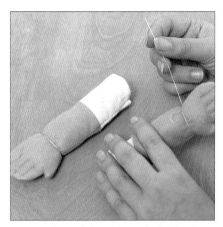

5 Hand-stitch lines through the hands to define the fingers. Wrap a strong thread round the wrist.

6 For the shoes, cut two pairs of side pieces and two sole pieces. Place each pair of side pieces right sides together and stitch the side seams. Sew the sole to the bottom edges of the sides.

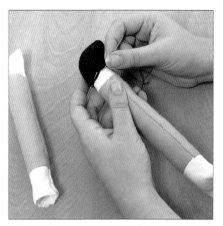

7 Stuff the leg pieces and the shoes with wadding, then stitch the lower edge of the leg to the upper edge of the shoe, turning under raw edges.

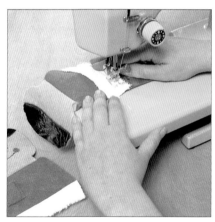

8 Cut out the torso pieces. Stitch the head pieces to the upper edge of the torso and the linen to the lower edge of the torso. Cut out one pocket and sew it in place on the front.

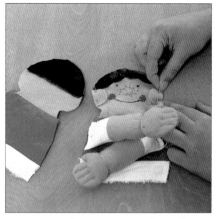

9 Cut out the ear pieces and pin, then sew them in position on either side of the head. Stitch the arms on either side of the torso. With right sides together, stitch the front of the body to the back all round the seam line. Turn through to the right side and stuff with wadding.

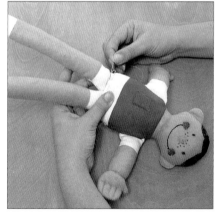

10 Tuck under the lower edges of the torso and hand-stitch the legs in place. Cut out the cap pieces and stitch them together. Cut out and make up the shorts. Sew the ribbon braces and buttons in place to finish.

JACKET

CREATED FROM ONE PIECE OF FELT, THIS EXTRAORDINARY JACKET HAS NO SEAMS AND IS ONLY CUT AT THE END OF THE PROCESS TO MAKE THE FRONT OPENING. SUCH COATS WERE ORIGINALLY MADE IN TURKEY AND IRAN BEFORE THEY EVOLVED INTO THE MUCH SIMPLER CAPES WORN BY SHEPHERDS. HEATHER BELCHER USED THE SAME TRADITIONAL SKILLS WHEN SHE MADE THIS UNIQUE CONTEMPORARY JACKET.

1 Draw the jacket shape onto a piece of calico then cut it out. Lay the carded slivers of fleece out on a flat surface. Make the first layer approximately 12.5 cm (5 in) larger than the calico shape, laying the white fleece so that the fibres run horizontally from wrist to wrist. Cover these with black fleece, laying the fibres at right angles to the white ones from neck to hem. Scatter soap flakes over the fleece and lay the calico shape on top.

2 Press down on the calico using the potato masher and pour some boiling water through the metal of the masher.

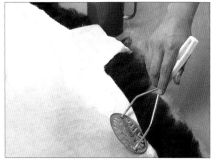

3 Work the water towards the edge of the calico but keep the uncovered edges of the fleece dry. Make the whole of the calico and the immediately underlying fleece wet in this way. Except for the neck, cuffs and hem, fold the uncovered edge of the black fleece over onto the calico shape resist.

4 Lay black fleece on top of the calico with the fibres running from neck to hem.

5 Lay white fleece to cover the black fleece with the fibres running from wrist to wrist. Turn the bottom layer of white fleece over onto the top layer. ▶

MATERIALS AND EQUIPMENT YOU WILL NEED

1.5 M (1½ YD) CALICO CLOTH • FABRIC MARKER • 750 G (1¾ LB) FLEECE IN CARDED SLIVERS, WHITE AND BLACK • SOAP FLAKES • POTATO MASHER • ROLLING PIN (OPTIONAL) • SCISSORS • BOWL • JUG • BUTTONS • NEEDLE AND MATCHING SEWING THREAD

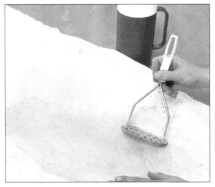

6 Scatter soap flakes over the surface and cover with a large piece of calico cloth. Pour boiling water through the potato masher onto the cloth and work the water towards the edges. Press and rub the fleece through the calico cloth to felt the wool. Once the felting process has started, you can roll a rolling pin across the surface to speed things up.

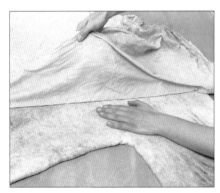

7 Carefully lift the calico cloth from the felt, using the flat of your hand to separate the fibres from the cloth.

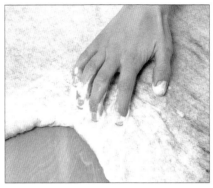

8 Continue to rub the felt with your hands, especially at the "seams", that is the folds in what is a continuous circle of felt.

9 Slip your hands between the felt and the calico to prevent the felt from sticking too firmly to the calico shape resist. Turn the piece over and work the other side in the same way.

10 Rub your hands along the "seams" to open them out and prevent them from forming ridges. When the felt feels strong and stable, carefully pull out the calico shape resist through the bottom of the jacket.

11 Cut the front opening of the jacket with scissors. Felt the jacket further and improve the shape by pummelling it with your hands. Rub the edges to make them strong and rounded while they are still soapy. Rinse the jacket in alternate hot and cold water and continue to work and pound the felt until the water runs clear of soap. Sew on the buttons and cut the button holes.

SLIPPERS

SHOE LINERS AND SLIPPERS MADE OF FELT ARE USED IN MANY COLD, SNOWY COUNTRIES. VERY WARM AND PRACTICALLY WATERPROOF IN DRY SNOW, THIS TYPE OF FOOTWEAR USED TO BE WORN BY CHILDREN AS BOOTS. HERE THEY ARE MADE TO ANY SIZE USING WELLINGTON BOOTS AS MOULDS BUT BY SUBSTITUTING YOUR OWN FEET AS THE MOULDS, YOU COULD MAKE YOURSELF A BESPOKE PAIR OF SLIPPERS TO AN EXACT FIT. ALTHOUGH THE INSTRUCTIONS MENTION ONLY ONE SLIPPER, WORK ON THE PAIR TOGETHER, COMPLETING EACH STEP FOR BOTH BEFORE MOVING ON TO THE NEXT.

1 Lay the teased-out carded blue fleece in a cross. Stand a wellington boot in the centre to check that you have enough wool to cover it. The bottom layer will become the outside of the boot. Remove the boot and place two layers of white fleece on top of the cross. Make them smaller than the cross and lay each layer at 90 degrees to the previous layer.

2 Place a smaller, rectangular layer of white fleece in the centre to make the sole thicker than the sides.

3 Dissolve soap flakes in boiling water to make a thick and slimy liquid; this is a more concentrated solution than for normal felting.

4 Place the fleece layers in a large shallow bowl and use the soap solution like glue to stick the fleece around the wellington boot.

5 Gently rub the fleece with your hands to start the felting process. As the fibres begin to mat, pour boiling water over the felt from time to time to rinse out the excess soap. Continue working and rinsing the fleece.

6 When the felt has begun to harden sufficiently, gently pull out the boot. ▶

MATERIALS AND EQUIPMENT YOU WILL NEED
FOR CHILD'S SIZE 5: 75 G (3 OZ) FLEECE IN CARDED SLIVERS, BLUE AND WHITE • SIZE 5 WELLINGTON BOOTS • SCISSORS • SOAP FLAKES • 2 BOWLS • DRESSMAKER'S PINS • NEEDLE AND MATCHING SEWING THREAD • SMALL FELT BALLS (OPTIONAL) • EMBROIDERY THREAD (OPTIONAL)

7 Gently slip your hand inside the slipper and work the felt, supporting the shape with your other hand. Patch any thin areas from the inside with extra fleece. Continue to work the felt until it is dense and strong and both slippers are equally felted. Rinse the slippers well and allow to dry.

8 When the felt is dry, neaten the tops of the slippers with scissors.

9 For the trim, pull off two thin strips of carded fleece approximately 1 m (1 yd) long. Dip these in hot, soapy water and rub your hand along the fibres to felt the strips.

10 Finish the felting by squeezing the fleece in your hands to keep the natural curl of the wool. Rinse while squeezing, then allow the wool to dry.

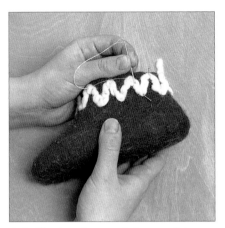

11 Pin the trim round the top of the slippers in a zigzag pattern leaving enough for a loop at the back. Stitch the trim in place with sewing thread.

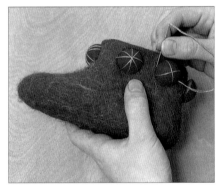

12 An alternative finish for the slippers is to make six small balls (see Basic Techniques) in a contrasting colour and stitch them in place with embroidery thread and decorative stitches.

PICTURE FRAME

THIS FRAME, DESIGNED BY SARAH RUBIE, CAN BE USED TO ENHANCE A SMALL HAND-PAINTED PICTURE, EMBROIDERY OR TAPESTRY. IT IS MADE USING COMMERCIAL FELT WHICH IS AVAILABLE IN A RANGE OF COLOURS. SPEND SOME TIME EXPERIMENTING WITH COLOURS, CHOOSING THEM CAREFULLY TO ENHANCE THE SUBJECT THEY WILL FRAME. IF YOU WISH TO HANG THE FRAME, STITCH A SMALL METAL RING TO THE BACK.

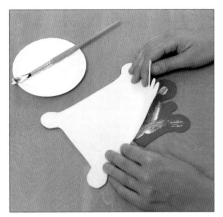

1 Make a card template for the main frame design. Using a vanishing fabric marker, trace round the template onto the vilene interfacing and a piece of commercial felt. Cut out the frame from the vilene and the felt and glue the two pieces together.

2 When the glue is dry, stitch round the edge of the frame with metallic thread using a sewing machine set to a fine satin stitch.

3 Lower the feed on the sewing machine and attach a darning foot. Complete the decoration inside the edge of the frame following the finished photograph.

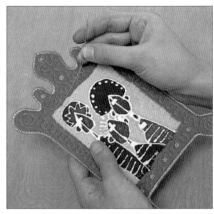

4 Neaten the edges of the picture with a hem using polyester thread. Stitch or glue your chosen image onto the middle of the frame.

MATERIALS AND EQUIPMENT YOU WILL NEED

PENCIL AND CARD • SCISSORS • VANISHING FABRIC MARKER • 10 x 12 CM (4 x 4¾ IN) VILENE INTERFACING •
10 x 12 CM (4 x 4¾ IN) COMMERCIAL FELT • FABRIC ADHESIVE AND GLUE BRUSH • METALLIC THREAD • SEWING MACHINE WITH DARNING FOOT •
POLYESTER THREAD • NEEDLE

HAT

THE RANDOM STRUCTURE OF FELT MAKES IT A PARTICULARLY GOOD FABRIC FOR MILLINERY. WHEN FELT IS WARM AND DAMP IT CAN BE PULLED IN ANY DIRECTION AND STEAM OR DIRECT HEAT WILL SHRINK IT. TO FORM A HAT, A SHAPE OR BLOCK IS NECESSARY. TRADITIONALLY THESE WERE MADE OF WOOD, BUT THEY ARE DIFFICULT TO FIND AND EXPENSIVE TO BUY SO YOU WILL HAVE TO IMPROVISE WITH HOUSEHOLD ITEMS. THIS HAT IS MADE FROM A CONE FELT HOOD AND A CAPELINE FELT HOOD AVAILABLE FROM MILLINERY WHOLESALER'S (SEE SUPPLIERS), BUT YOU COULD STRIP DOWN AND RESHAPE AN OLD FELT HAT.

1 Select a suitable heatproof bowl to use as the hat block and a smaller bowl which must fit, upturned, inside the larger bowl. This will raise the larger bowl up off the work surface allowing it to be spun round and worked on from all sides. The teapot lid will sit on top.

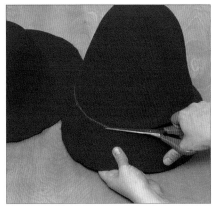

2 The cone-shaped felt hood is too deep for the crown of the hat so cut off approximately 12.5 cm (5 in) from the rim and set this aside to use as a hat band.

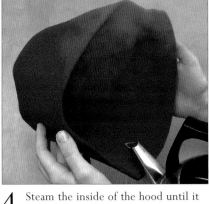

4 Steam the inside of the hood until it is warm, damp and soft. You should use a kettle that will sit on the hob (i.e. not an electric one). This will supply a steady amount of steam.

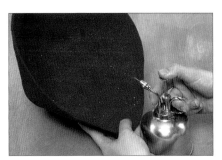

3 Use the plant mister to spray the inside of the hood with warm water.

MATERIALS AND EQUIPMENT YOU WILL NEED

2 HEATPROOF BOWLS, 1 HEAD SIZED, 1 TO FIT INSIDE • TEAPOT LID • CONE-SHAPED FELT HOOD • SCISSORS • PLANT MISTER • KETTLE • STEAM IRON • STRING • CAPELINE FELT HOOD • SHARP KNIFE • TAILOR'S CHALK • TACKING THREAD • NEEDLE AND MATCHING SEWING THREAD • TAPE MEASURE

5 Push the teapot lid up into the centre of the hood. Use a hot iron to soften the felt above it, then mould it to the shape of the lid.

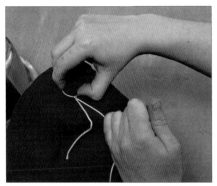

6 Secure the felt in place with string. Make a slip knot and wind the string tightly round the shape of the lid.

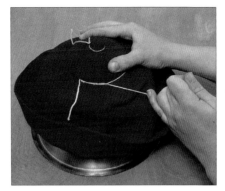

7 Place the lid on top of the upturned bowl and pull the felt over the lower part of the lid. Use the hot iron to help stretch the felt over the curve and shrink it in under the lid. Tie string round to hold the shape.

8 Using the plant mister and steam from the kettle, damp down the felt with warm water. Pull the felt down evenly over the bowl. Use the hot iron to help define the shape of the rim.

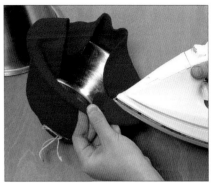

9 Lift the bowl up and turn the felt underneath. Press it dry with the iron and cut away the excess felt gathered up inside the bowl. Allow the felt to dry on the bowl.

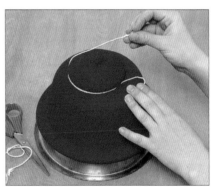

10 When the felt is completely dry remove the string. If you remove it before the felt is completely dry, the hat will lose its shape. ▶

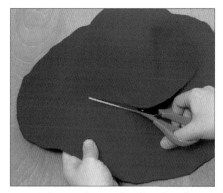

11 Stab into the capeline hood with a sharp knife to make a starting hole. Cut out with scissors and discard the middle, leaving the brim. (The discarded felt could be used to make a cap.)

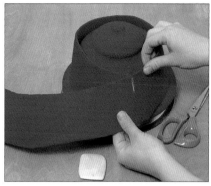

13 Press the felt cut off which was set aside in step 2. Wrap it round the crown and mark a cutting line with tailor's chalk. Remove the band and cut it to the correct length and width.

15 Place the brim beneath the crown and tack it in place. Mark out the cutting line for the brim, measuring from the crown to the edge and marking all round with tailor's chalk. Cut along the line to neaten the brim. Trim away any excess felt inside the hat, too. Sew the brim firmly to the crown with strong stab stitches and remove the tacking stitches. If you wish, trim the hat with felt off-cuts or a felt brooch.

12 Dampen the felt for the brim and press it flat with the iron. Allow it to dry flat.

14 Butt the two cut edges of the hat band together and tack in place. The band should be a snug fit over the hat. When you are satisfied with the fit, sew the ends of the band together and remove the tacking stitches.

TEMPLATES

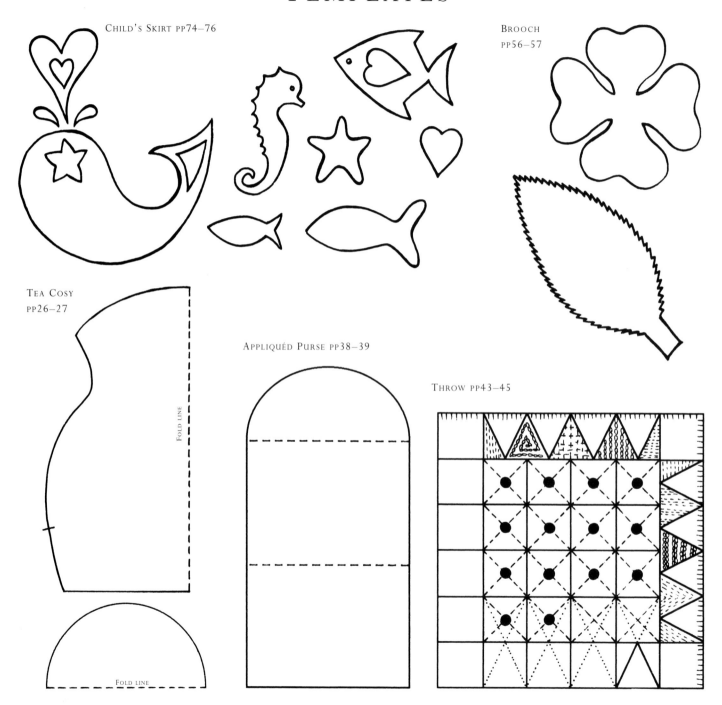

CHILD'S SKIRT PP74–76

BROOCH
PP56–57

TEA COSY
PP26–27

FOLD LINE

FOLD LINE

APPLIQUÉD PURSE PP38–39

THROW PP43–45

DOLL PP77–79

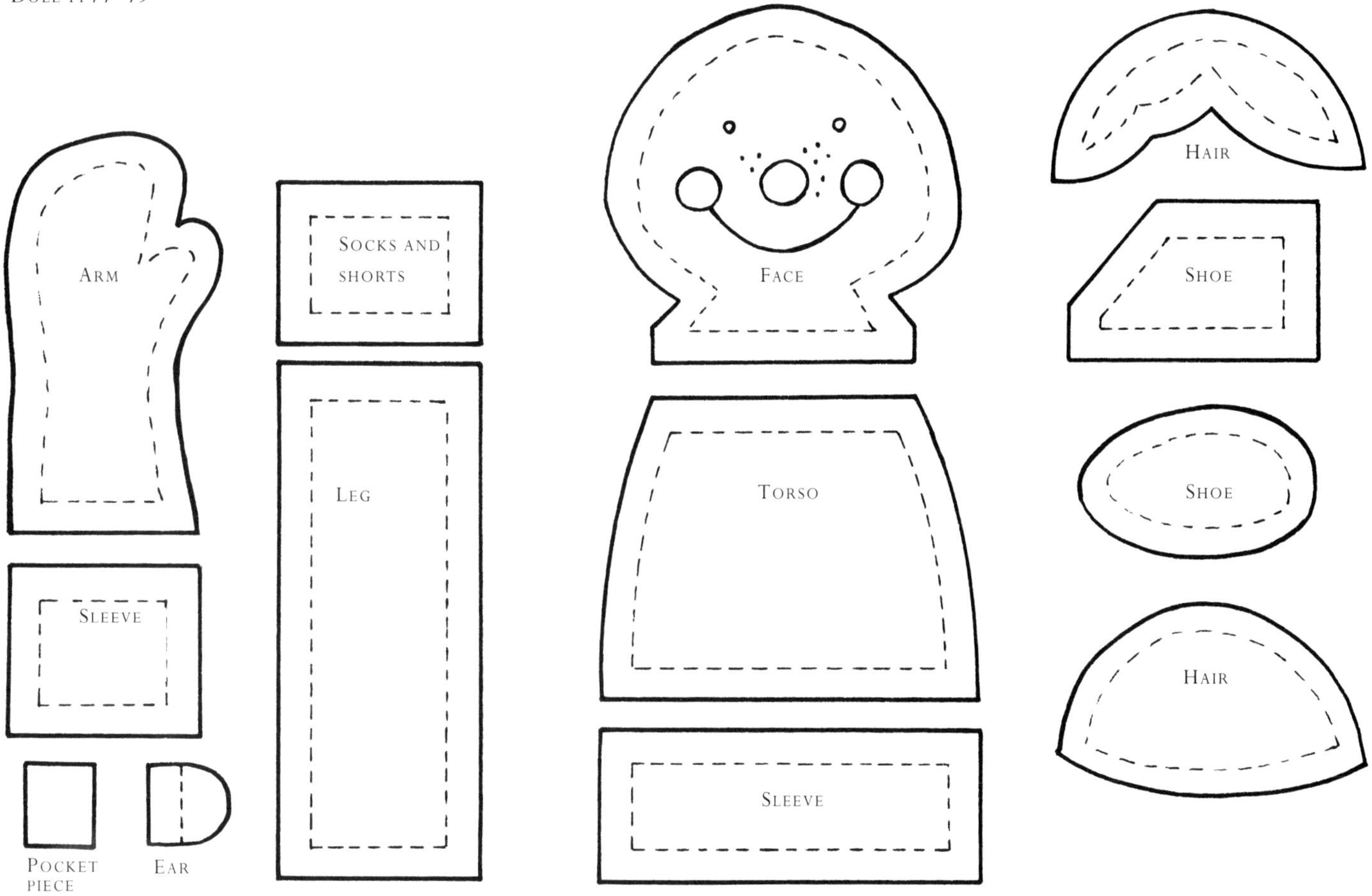

ARM

SOCKS AND SHORTS

LEG

SLEEVE

POCKET PIECE

EAR

FACE

TORSO

SLEEVE

HAIR

SHOE

SHOE

HAIR

CHILD'S CARDIGAN PP70–73

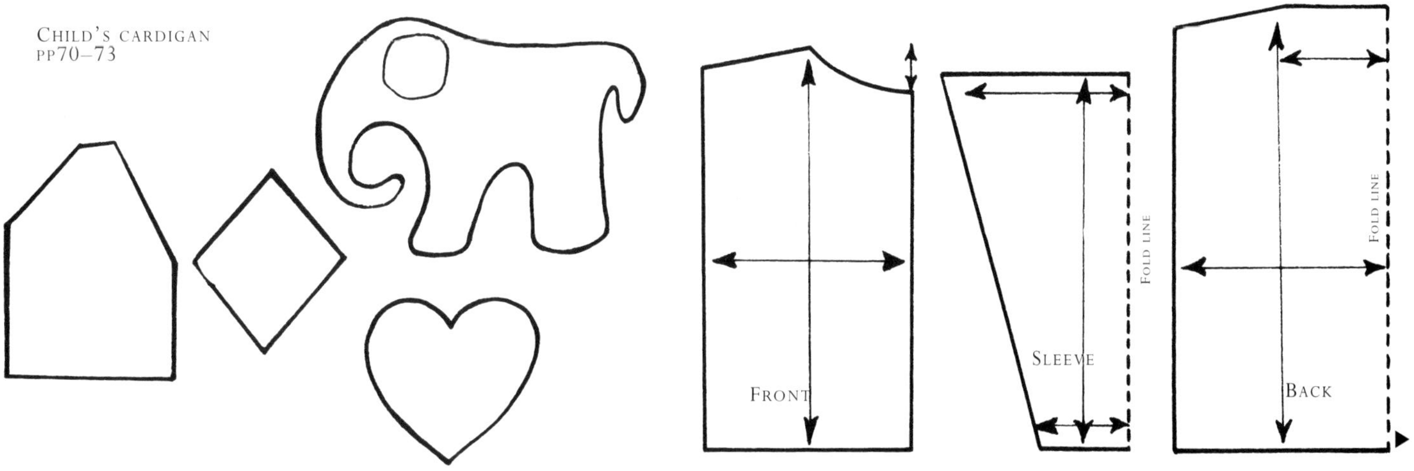

FRONT

SLEEVE

FOLD LINE

BACK

FOLD LINE

CACTUS CURTAIN PP60–62

SUPPLIERS

United Kingdom

Adeleide Walker
2 Mill Yard Workshops
Otley Mill
Ilkley Road
Otley
West Yorkshire LS21 3JP
(wool fibres)

B Brown
79–89 Pentonville Road
London N1 9LW
*(commercial felt cut to length –
branches also in Birmingham,
Bristol, Glasgow, Hemel Hempstead
and Leeds)*

Boon and Lane
7–11 Taylor Street
Luton
Bedfordshire
(hat blocks)

Catherine Delaney
Unit 6
The Chandlery
50 Westminster Bridge Road
London SE1 7QY
(cone and capeline felt hoods)

Fibrecrafts
Style Cottage
Lower Eashing
Godalming
Surrey GU7 2QD
(dyes, fleece, hand and drum carders)

The Handweavers Studio and
Gallery Ltd
29 Haroldstone Road
London E17 7AN
(dyes, fleece and yarns)

Hayes Chemicals
55–57 Gledgall Road
London SE15
(dyes, Glauber salts)

Hedgehog Equipment
Meodene
Broadway Road
Mickleton
Glos GL55 6PT
(hand and drum carders)

Kemtex Services Ltd
Tameside Business Park
Windmill Lane
Denton
Manchester M34 3QS
(dyes)

M & R Dyes
Carters
Station Road
Wickham Bishop
Witham
Essex CM8 3JB
(dyes)

Paul Craig Ltd
Unit 32
Wealden Business Park
Farmingham Road

Crowborough
East Sussex TN6 2RJ
(cone and capeline felt hoods)

Canada

Abbey Arts & Crafts
4118 Hastings Street
Burnaby
B. C.
(fleece and hoods)

Curries
155 The Queensway East
Mississauga
Ontario
(fleece)

Dresew
337 West Hastings Street
Vancouver
B. C.
(sewing materials)

Dundee Hobby Crafts
1518–6551 No 3 Road
Richmond
B. C.
*(various feltwork and sewing
materials)*

Fun Craft City Ltd
13890 104 Avenue
Surrey
B. C.
*(fleece, commercial felt and sewing
materials)*

Lewis Craft
2300 Younge Street
Toronto
Ontario
(hoods, fleece and commercial felt)

Michaels (Arts and Crafts
Superstore)
200 North Service Road
Oaksville Town Centre 2
Oaksville
Ontario
*(fleece, commercial felt, hoods and
sewing materials)*

New Zealand

Butterwick (LZ) Ltd
34–38 Kalmia Street
Ellerslie
Auckland

Pan Pacific Marketing Ltd
38 Ronia Road
Mt Roskill
Auckland

Australia

Lincraft
tel: (03) 9875 7575
(stores in every capital)

Spotlight
tel: freecall 1800 500 021
(60 stores throughout)

INDEX